Trumpet Sounds

A CALL OF WARNING AND REPENTENCE

Rory Larsen

TRILOGY CHRISTIAN PUBLISHERS

TUSTIN, CA

TRILOGY

Trilogy Christian Publishers
A Wholly Owned Subsidary of Trinity Broadcasting Network
2442 Michelle Drive
Tustin, CA 92780

For information, address Trilogy Christian Publishing

Rights Department, 2442 Michelle Drive, Tustin, Ca 92780.

Trilogy Christian Publishing/ TBN and colophon are trademarks of Trinity Broadcasting Network.

For information about special discounts for bulk purchases, please contact Trilogy Christian Publishing.

Manufactured in the United States of America

10 9 8 7 6 5 4 3 2 1

Library of Congress Cataloging-in-Publication Data is available.
ISBN 978-1-63769-106-9
ISBN 978-1-63769-107-6 (ebook)

Contents

Dedication

I would like to dedicate this book to my beautiful wife Takysia. She is the one person that gave me the courage to believe and trust the Holy Spirit inside of me. Without her encouragement throughout the years, this moment would not have been possible. She has been my counselor, confidante, and best friend.

Preface

As I sensed the call of God to pen the words of this book I felt an overwhelming awareness of my own inadequacy and simultaneously the urgency of His message. As I have continued to yield to the Spirit's call, those feelings have intensified as I have consumed His Word and truly His Word has consumed me. His Word has become sweet as honey in my mouth, yet bitter to my stomach.

It has taken me, I am embarrassed to say, an extremely long time to yield to and obey Him in this call that I long to accomplish. It is my desire to be a shofar for God, the proverbial ram's horn. The shofar has many interesting characteristics, but what intrigues me the most is that it is a perfect picture of what God desires from this book and quite frankly from both you and me.

The shofar or ram's horn is only good for its heavenly purpose if it is detached from its earthly host. In order for that to occur the ram must be completely dead.

It can only serve the Master's purpose if it is hollow and empty of personal residue and is held in the Master's hand. Then and only then can it perform it's intended purpose of a yielded conduit to the breath of the Trumpeter, God Almighty Himself.

> *I was in the Spirit on the Lord's Day, and I heard behind me a loud voice, as of a trumpet, saying, I am the Alpha and the Omega, the First and the Last, and, what you see, write in a book...Write the things which you have seen, and the things which are, and the things which will take place after this.*
>
> Revelation 1:11, 19

One of the main purposes of the shofar blast is to alert God's people. Sometimes it is a blast heard as a coronation pronouncing kingship. Other blasts signify a call to repentance and yet another blast is meant to awaken the soul to God's intended determinations. Many times, the shofar blast is meant to sound an alarm of warning to wake up God's people to God's purposes before it is too late.

The intention of this book is to do just that. To proclaim the lordship of Jesus Christ, and it is a call to repentance. Hopefully it serves as an earth-shattering awakening to your soul as it has been to mine.

Blow the Trumpet

"Warn them of My judgments
And of impending doom
Or else unexpectedly
They will see the Bridegroom"

With all of the many "prophetic instruments" heralding their voices today, especially given the intense fascination and preoccupation with end-time scenarios, I am convinced today more than ever that it is time to answer the call of God's word and, "Blow the ram's horn trumpet in Zion!" (Joel 2:15 MSG)

It is time for God's people to hear the divine shofar and echo the sound heaven is making with our own instruments to awaken a nation and call her to repentance and simultaneously heighten the spiritual awareness of the body of Christ to prepare.

The finger of God has drawn a line in the sand, and we have taken our national foot and brushed it away as if to smugly say to God Almighty, "I don't care about your opinion!"

It appears we have done more than just step over a line drawn in the sand; we have challenged His sole right and authority to set the boundaries that that line represents. We have become a godless, self-sufficient, arrogant people who have somehow concluded that God will continue to be longsuffering toward this nation's sin perpetually.

George Mason said at the 1787 Constitutional Convention, "As nations cannot be rewarded or punished in the next world, so they must be in this. By an inevitable chain of causes and effects. Providence punishes national sins by national calamities."

The United States has already suffered multiple national calamities which, for all intents and purposes, have borne little true fruit of repentance. We are reaching critical mass on the calamity scale and we will continue to experience national calamities like a steady staccato beat of a drum until the final gong is sounded. This book serves as the precursor accompaniment note blowing through a watchman's shofar, meant to herald a clear clarion call to repentance, renewal, and preparation. We are not only living in the last days, but we are about to experience the final moments of a nation.

We are living in a day of easy listening. We are fortunate enough to be living in a nation that at any given moment we can turn on the television, radio, or smart phone app and listen to a myriad of gospel presentations. The multitude of easy listening devices are serving as a substitute for hearing the voice of the Lord individually and serves as a mistress to the divine relationship with the voice of God. We listen to all sorts of uncertain sounds proclaiming a message that we mimic and yet have no sure word from the Lord of our own.

Where are the true watchmen with the sure word from God? The true watchman, the genuine men and women of God called to warn of impending judgment for sin, thundering the requirements for revival and renewal?

Today within the body of Christ there is this unseen cloud of doom that is being sensed and even felt by the ungodly and unconverted. Where are the trumpet sounds that are bellowing heaven's voice of warning? Where are the men and women of God willing to allow their shofar to blow and reverberate through them as a sound that is the very breath of God, which will serve to bring this nation to its knees in repentance?

There are some who would claim this mantle of watchman or prophet and wear it as a cloak of importance while all along they sit and simply echo some book or author instead of truly reverberating the sound of heavens voice that they hear for themselves. You see we read the spiritual prognosticators and echo their "revelation" as if it is our very own becoming parrots instead of prescient, impersonator instead of seer, plagiarist instead of prophet.

But what is heaven saying...to you? What does His Word say...to you? We are called to be watchmen with shofars made of marbled iron, an invincible messenger with an indestructible, irrepressible message. Instead we copy and paste messages from one another in an attempt to remove the blood from our own hands.

But in order to have the clean hands that Ezekiel speaks of, we too must have the personal word from God released from within our own spirits and spoken through our own lips and then and only then will we have unbloodied hands.

> *Then He said to me: "Son of man, go to the house of Israel and speak with My words to them..." Moreover, He said to me: "Son of man, receive into your heart all My words that I speak to you, and hear with your ears. And go, get to the captives, to the children of your people, and speak to them and tell them, 'Thus says the Lord God.'"*
> Ezekiel 3:4, 10–11

God has a word that He wants to speak through you. It is not a regurgitated word from some book or sermon that you heard or read. He has a word that He wants you to hear and share because you have spent personal time with Him and not try and share something that you are reiterating from another.

You are a true watchman when you get on your knees and you stay there until you get close enough to God to hear the wings of the living creatures rubbing together. Genuine personal time spent in heaven by the Spirit of God waiting for all of heaven to become silent so Jesus can whisper His breath of prophetic utterance that will not only deliver your soul but also those that hear it as it flows through you. Unless and until your messages come directly from His Holy Spirit because you have spent unhurried intimacy with Jesus Christ than you are still just a parrot with blood on its hands.

Here is the call of God going out to "him who has an ear."

> *Son of man, I have made you a watchman for the house of Israel; therefore hear a word from My mouth, and give them warning from me: When I say to the wicked, "You shall surely die," and you give him no warning, nor speak to warn the wicked from his wicked way, to save his life, that same wicked man shall die in his iniquity, but his blood I will require at your hand, Yet, if you warn the wicked, and he does not turn from his wickedness, nor from his wicked way, he shall die in his iniq-*

uity; but you have delivered your soul. Again, when a righteous man turns from his righteousness and commits iniquity, and I lay a stumbling block before him, he shall die; because you did not give him warning, he shall die in his sin, and his righteousness which he has done shall not be remembered; but his blood I will require at your hand. Nevertheless, if you warn the righteous man that the righteous should not sin, and he does not sin, he shall surely live because he took warning; also you will have delivered your soul.

Ezekiel 3:17–21

For all of those multitudes of individuals feeling this impending doom hovering in the air over the United States and sensing that something unspeakable is about to happen. Without a true watchman sounding heaven's specific alarm they will fall for every headline extrapolation touting to know the future. *In the absence of a true prophetic word of the Lord, the world and the church will fall for any repetitive declaration because it satisfies that unknowing even if it isn't the truth.*

God forbid that we allow this opportunity of heart searching that the world and the church is going through right now to be satisfied with something mixed with speculation and lose the opportunity to fill that void with a pure word from the throne of God. The only way for that to occur is to not only spend more intimate time with Jesus personally, but to also allow His Word to penetrate you deeply.

If you listen very carefully, you can hear the sound of the angels tuning their trumpets. Echo that sound!

Allow His message to flow through you like the breath that runs through the shofar. Heaven right now is making trumpet sounds, but can you hear it? Blow that trumpet! Sound an alarm! Allow the breath of God to flow through you to an anxious uncertain world and proclaim the heart of Jesus Christ.

Trumpet Sounds

Man of God I'm calling you
Who are you to be?
An Instrument of the Almighty
Or a ram's horn who flees?

"Son of man, I have made you a watchman for the house of Israel; therefore hear a word from My mouth, and give them warning from Me" (Ezek. 3:17).

The remainder of these writings will be answering the call of the watchman to sound an alarm. The blowing of this shofar (the writing of this book) is answering the call to echo the breath of God sounding through an instrument of death (me) to bring both alarm and hope.

Alarm because this nation is about to undergo drastic changes in the form of judgment and hope because through that judgment there will be a remnant people that will experience true revival as never before in the history of the United States.

In the passage of scripture above, Ezekiel was challenged like most men called of God to speak the truth to a rebellious people. In God's statement to Ezekiel, there is an implicit and explicit statement being conveyed to the prophet. The underlying implication is a question. "Ezekiel, what have I made you for?" And then God goes on to explicitly answer the very question he implies. "I have made you a watchman...therefore, hear a word from My mouth and give them warning from Me."

The exact same challenge is going out today. God has a word that He wants to speak directly from His mouth to the watchman's ear. It is a divine call to listen to the trumpet voice of God and duplicate or echo what you hear with a confidently magnified amplification of His voice. Even more than that though, He desires something other than just a mimicking of the sound that is heard but He is yearning for the transference of His heart.

Anybody can get up and repeat a prophetic message but only one who transfers the heart of God is worthy to unleash the trumpet sound as intended. There is a lot of parroting of the prophetic voice today. Somebody crafts a well-written proclamation and the majority of its readers parrot the writer without actually conveying the full intent of God's heart. A true prophetic message is one that is birthed in prayer comes directly from

God and is conveyed with the pathos received from the transference from the heart of God.

Just as you can play an instrument and not convey the emotional impact of a piece of music, so too can a prophetic word come forth without the full impact of the author's intent when there is no heartfelt connection to the song. There must be a heartfelt connection to the subject matter and that cannot happen by repeating another man's revelation. That can only happen by connecting with the One who holds the future.

There was once a young man who moved from his homeland in Germany to live on the beautiful mountain tops of the Swiss Alps. Since he was new to the area, he spent much of his time alone and wandering the trails of the mountains. One day during his explorations, he stumbled upon an elderly gentleman who befriended the young boy and tried to mentor him with ideas to help acclimate him to his new environment.

One day the elderly man gave him a piece of original sheet music that he had written twenty years prior and allowed him to play and practice on his personal alphorn. With just a few instructions, the young man took very quickly to the playing of this instrument.

Day after day, the young boy would practice until his lips were sore, and day after day he struggled to really hear or enjoy the piece he was attempting to play. Finally, after much discouragement over the resulting sounds and much practice the young man admitted to his friend that he really did not think he was capable of playing this instrument and especially this particular piece of music.

The elderly man said, "Play the piece for me and allow me to critique your work."

The young boy played the piece from beginning to end and the elderly man's response was resounding silence.

Finally, the young man said, "Well? What do you think?"

The elderly man replied, "I have to admit my boy, it does sound like you are stepping on a group of ducks and causing them extreme pain."

They both had a hearty laugh and after several moments, the elderly man said, "Let me tell you the story of this song."

"Thirty years ago, I was walking these trails with the love of my life, my new bride, my wife. As we walked the trails, we spoke of our dreams, our future together, and discussed our many plans and hopes for our life. As we walked, my fair lady slipped on the path and tumbled twenty feet down the mountain, hitting her head on a large stone. She left me that day for the afterlife.

"My boy, this piece of music was the captured result of my anguished heart and the loss that I suffered on that day." He continued to express the specifics of how deep his love was for his bride and then after much reminiscing he stopped and said, "Here my boy, allow me to play the piece as it was intended."

As he began to gently blow the air from his lungs into the alphorn, the sound that came out had a haunting, melancholy effect.

As he breathed the last note, a tear gently fell from his cheek and he handed the instrument back to the young man who by this time had tears streaming down his face.

"Now I know," said the young man, his words breaking through this emotional epiphany. "Now I know the difference between stepping on ducks and actually breathing out the intention of the author's heart."

Are you a duck walker or are you breathing out the intention of the Author's heart? A true watchman doesn't just blow indistinguishable breaths through the shofar. It's not just an echo but the transference of the very heart of God.

A true watchman conveys more than just an annoying superficial sound through the headpiece of a dead animal. A true watchman sees the coming storm, but he not only announces the coming calamity, he also delivers an emotional alarm that conveys the heartfelt concern from the author of the message. It's not enough to just blow uncertain sounds but we must capture and release the heart of God.

"Hear a word from My mouth..." God has a message that must be proclaimed with the pathos of Calvary. Judgment is coming to this nation and His heart is broken over it. He does not release one blow of judgment in anger; on the contrary, He weeps with every consequential hammer strike. God has a warning that must be proclaimed by his watchmen, but a true watchman is distinguished from all other instrumentalists because he has a tear falling from his cheek as he releases each breath of warning from the very heart of God.

If you progress through the pages of this book, I can't promise you that it will be easy reading, but what I can promise you is that it will be intense, emotional, exciting, frightening, hopeful, and promising.

Each message of warning that blows through this watchman onto these pages is more than a mere recitation of sheet music; it is an attempt to release the fully affected heart of God.

Tornado Dream

Blow the ram's horn
The Lord's Shofar
To proclaim His holy Word
And to show them "Therefore"

For all this His anger is not turned away, but His
hand is stretched out still. For the people do not
turn to Him who strikes them, nor do they seek the
Lord of Hosts. Therefore the Lord will cut off head
and the tail from Israel, Palm branch and bulrush
in one day.

Isaiah 9:12–14

This scripture speaks to a nation who has been afflicted by calamity after calamity after calamity and yet they still do not turn to the Lord in true repentance. They sense that the hand of God is striking them as a nation and yet the scripture says they do not seek Him who strikes them. *"Therefore* the Lord will cut off the head and the tail..." This is a true picture of the condition that the United States is in at this very moment.

The United States has been under a measure of judgment for years. Judgment is not coming, it is here! Just like Pharaoh of old we are in denial that the mighty hand of God is already upon us. I fear we too will not recognize His hand until the firstborn are smitten. God help us!

Even secular prognosticators can see and are pronouncing impending doom. They don't truly know the horrible fate that awaits us, but they can sense something is about to happen and, in their fear and paranoia announce guestimates of consequential returns for our actions and activities. We are now hearing everything from an EMP attack to a solar flare disruption of the electrical grid to the collapse of the dollar and hyperinflation.

Much of this could very well happen, but at the same time, most of it is pure speculation in order to garner a modicum of control of an impending uncontrollable. It brings a measure of peace if somebody can appear to know what is about to happen and be rushing to prepare for it.

The truth is more along the lines that nobody truly knows what awaits this nation but God, and God is hollering through a gentle whisper but nobody is listening. What awaits this nation is what the scripture declares. *For all this His anger is not turned away, but His hand is stretched out still. For the people do not turn to Him who strikes them, nor do they seek the Lord of Hosts. Therefore the Lord will cut off head and the tail...*

For the people do not turn to Him who strikes them. We turn to newscasters, tabloids, and Hollywood. We listen to every politician, talk-show host or voice proclaiming the future of our nation, but we rarely turn to hear His voice. Many times, we listen to these false teachers and prophets telling lies and proclaiming a false sense of security when the Holy Spirit is whisper-screaming and yet we don't hear Him. We turn to everyone but Him.

It has become so clear now that God's hand is stretched out against this nation that it doesn't take a prophet to see it and yet...*the people do not turn to Him who strikes them.* It is undeniable now that even the Cataract Christians are unsettled over what's about to happen and yet we do not seek the Lord. The scripture says that when any people are in this state, a "Therefore" must occur.

Therefore the Lord will cut off head and the tail...

There is coming a series of judgments that will align with this proclamation of scripture, "the Lord will cut off head and the tail..." Because we recognize and sense that we are under His hand of judgment and we still have not turned to Him, He has unleashed a judgment that has and will cut off the head and the tail.

The time has come, and you will begin to see it in further gradual increments before the completed judgment falls but make no mistake, judgement is here. The head and the tail that the scripture is referring to has a two-fold meaning for our nation. First it is our political system (the head) and the news media (the tail) and secondly it is referring to our nation as a whole. East Coast (head) and West Coast (tail) and judgment is here from the East Coast to the West Coast and it will impact the entirety of our country.

Isaiah tells us specifically who the head and the tail are. He doesn't leave us to speculate but specifically defines who they are and what the next series of judgments will be upon them.

"The elder and honorable, he is the head; The prophet who teaches lies he is the tail" (Is. 9:15). Our political system is the elder and honorable head that is about to be cut off and the news media is the prophet who teaches lies, they are the tail that is about to be severed.

What once was a nation full of life with an honorable leadership structure, the head. It also had a fully-functioning body, the people. And lastly, it has a tail fully attached and following along with "truth-awareness," the media. All have experienced a splitting or an undoing of their collective existence, and now both the head and the tail not only operate alone, but both are agonizing over this fatal blow and are trying to reattach itself to the body for control.

This amputation has occurred to both systems and in "one day" (vs. 14) virtually overnight both have had their connective tissues cut off, from not only each other but the rest of its body. The politicians once experienced cordial favor no matter which side of the political spectrum won an election, and now a severing has occurred, and the people are awakened by the pain of this severing and the peace that was once experienced between the political parties no longer exists and this is itself a judgment from God. Victorious existence no longer exists.

The news media is also experiencing a displacement from the people. What once was a symbiotic relationship with the head has now become a non-cooperative and hateful existence upon this separation from the people, and make no mistake the body feels this separation as well and the loyalty with which the tail once had from the body that has been cut off.

This scripture speaks a proclamation of a striking blow that severs the two institutions from each other, but they are also severed from its body, the people which gives them both life. This verse is speaking to a total system split that suffers a distinct slice to their livelihoods, their peace, and their unification as it exists and it will alter their presence forever. When scripture says God is going to cut off the head and the tail, it is speaking not only to the existence but also to its subsistence as a whole.

What exactly does that mean? What specifically is going to happen? A severing, and it has already happened. The body (the people) are squirming in its separated state with no political leadership and no true news media word that can be trusted! A severing has already taken place, but few see it. Everybody is going about being enamored by tales of fanciful interpretations and yet nobody is crying out to God for mercy and repentance.

Make no mistake the landscape of this nation is about to undergo dramatic change. Judgment is coming across this land and the political system is about to be "cut off" in the words of scripture, from the people, its body. A news media tail will also be separated from its body and they will no longer exist in their current form. The elder and the lying prophet are about to be judged, and they won't recognize it as they both squirm like a snake after the death strike with an axe to both the head and the tail.

We are watching this judgment play out before our very eyes every day. The head (politicians) squirming and writhing around in their amputation and the tail (news media) flailing about for attention. The two desperately need each other and yet they continue in their disunity not knowing that they are an object lesson for God's judgment.

The second part of this verse is key to understanding the resultant outcome of this severing of the head and tail. *Therefore the Lord will cut off head and the tail from Israel, palm branch and bulrush in one day.* The palm branch in this instance represents victory and peace and the bulrush represents their platform.

The politicians (the elder and honorable) will continue to see disputed victories in their elections with no peaceful resolutions to bring the two sides together. The palm branch is cut off from the head, and it is God's doing. It is a disruption to their victories and their peace

The news media (the prophet who teaches lies) will see their medium or their means of message transference and it will also be cut off. The people are beginning to see the truth that they are *all* "prophets that teach lies." The lying prophets' methods of messaging will be cut off because the people will separate themselves from the lies as they are exposed. The life that the tail once imbued from the body (the people) will gradually be emptied of its force with only a skeleton remaining. God is exposing the news media, both sides of the opinionated spectrum for who they truly are, *lying prophets.*

Both head and tail will suffer a death blow from this severing of the life-flow from its body the people. Politicians will struggle to victory like in no other age, the divisions of the people will make it nearly impossible for politicians to claim clear victory. The media monster will suffer credibility issues on both sides of the political spectrum and will slowly slither around until death finally swallows them up, until one day they financially slither away from their platforms. This judgment is already taking place but the culmination of it will be a sight to behold.

There is a dual interpretation to this prophetic portion of scripture, and Isaiah speaks to a people who won't acknowledge their condition before a holy God and he speaks to a nation whose judgment is coming to both controlling borders. For America that means the West Coast and the East Coast.

There is a severing storm coming to both coasts of America. A storm so great that she comes apart and has to go in opposite directions like a tornado splitting in two.

The start of my journey with this writing began with a dream. I don't normally remember my dreams but when I do they are usually, like everyone else's dreams, the mind's attempt to process the events of the day or week etc. I would say that it's rare for me to receive a dream or a vision from the Holy Spirit, but after this dream, He began to download the accompanying revelations within the writings of this book. I don't particularly put too much stock in dreams or visions unless they can be strenuously and vigorously backed up by scripture.

The dream that I had was as follows. I was sitting inside of a house which I did not recognize but it must have been mine because I could sense that my family was with me and even though I did not see any of them as the dream progressed I could sense them there and I spoke to them as the dream unfolded.

There was a terrible storm approaching. It seemed like one of those ominous black Iowa thunderstorms. You could literally feel this unsettling as the atmosphere changed and you could sense this impending doom. The sky was black, and the clouds were rolling in. As I viewed this approaching storm, I walked out on the front porch and started yelling at all of the people outside oblivious to what was fast approaching behind them. I was screaming and motioning with my arm to run and take shelter before it's too late and everybody just ignored me as if they couldn't hear anything I was saying or see me motioning to them at all.

Suddenly a giant funnel cloud began to form directly in front of me. Swirling and dark and menacing and it grew quick with intensity, suddenly the tornado sirens began to sound and all of the people that I had just been yelling at took notice and began to run and try to escape this angry twisting cloud. I remember stepping back inside the house and saying in exasperation, "Now they listen, now that it's too late."

As I watched, the people began to scatter for safety and then suddenly this giant twister split into two separate and distinct tornadoes. Keep in mind this did not split in half into two smaller tornadoes, it was as if they split into an exact mirror of each other. Now there were two terrifying tornadoes. Just as rapidly as they had split into a mirror image of themselves, one went to the West and the other to the East.

I awakened from this dream with a dreadful awareness that this was from the Holy Spirit and He was giving warning of what is to come. The United States of America is about to be judged as a nation and it will begin on the coasts both West and East and will impact not only the entire country but will ripple into the entire continent and the effects will be felt worldwide.

The West Coast will soon experience what I will call a Water Judgment. For years people have been predicting "The Big One," so much so that most residents are numb to the foretelling of it. The big one of course is an earthquake that will devastate the coast like none other in it's past. While I am sure much of the predictions over the years have been half-truths and half paranoia, what is coming will pale in comparison to any imagination yet to be forecasted.

> *And as it was in the days of Noah, so it will be also in the days of the Son of Man; "They ate, they drank, they married wives, they were given in marriage, until the day that Noah entered the ark, and the flood came and destroyed them all.*
>
> Luke 17:26–27

Just as in the days of Noah, there will one day come a beautiful spring day and people will be going about their lives, oblivious to the peril just ahead of them. There will be a foursome on the golf course about to tee off, there will be a couple standing at the altar at an outside wedding beginning to say their "I do's," and there will be several joggers running down the beach on a beautiful sunny spring day. When suddenly, one of the runners will glance down at her Fit-Bit and the time will read 3:57 p.m. and unexpectedly the ground will begin to rumble. As it gains in intensity, it will seem as if the very sky is shaking with the ground.

The results will be devastating, the "Big One" will be the "Last One" because this shaking will be like nothing ever experienced heretofore. This shaking will launch a giant tsunami that will devastate the entire West Coast and it will happen suddenly and without warning. In one hour, it will all be over and in one hour the devastation will have just begun.

> *Likewise as it was also in the days of Lot: They ate, they drank, they bought, they sold, they planted, they built; but on the day that Lot went out of Sodom it rained fire and brimstone from heaven and destroyed them all. Even so will it be in the day when the Son of Man is revealed.*
>
> Luke 17:28–30

Likewise, just as in the days of Lot, people will be going about doing their daily lives. Selling hot dogs on the street corners, building skyscrapers, and suddenly in one hour, the East Coast will experience Fire Judgment. A nuclear holocaust that burns with intense heat will swiftly come and devastate the East Coast.

Water Judgment on the West Coast and Fire Judgment on the East Coast.

Why this judgment to the coasts of America? Do you suppose that Californians are worse than Iowans? Are New Yorkers worse than Floridians? No, a hundred times no! God is not judging this nation as some suppose because there is a large number of homosexuals in San Francisco. He doesn't judge Nevada because of prostitution or gambling. I know that I take a risk and some will sit in their piousness and think that this judgment is somehow because the residents on the coasts are somehow worse than the rest of us.

But I ask you, worse than who? Worse than Iowans or South Dakotans who allow the murdering of babies in legalized death clinics? Worse than Floridians or Coloradoans who sit around the water or on mountain-tops enjoying their legalized drug use?

> *And Jesus answered and said to them, "Do you suppose that these Galileans were worse sinners than all other Galileans, because they suffered such things? I tell you, no; but unless you repent you will all likewise perish.*
>
> Luke 13:2–3

Worse than Minnesotans or Illinoisans who have outlawed prayer in the schools? No, no, no a thousand times no!

> *Or those eighteen on whom the tower in Siloam fell and killed them, do you think that they were worse sinners than all other men who dwelt in Jerusalem? I tell you, no; but unless you repent you will all likewise perish.*
>
> Luke 13:4–5

The judgment that is coming is not a judgment on the specific "sins" of the people per se. It is a judgment on a nation that has turned her back on God and the rain will fall on the just and the unjust. This is not a judgment solely on the coasts of this country, the effects of this will be felt throughout the entire nation.

What begins as Water Judgment on the West Coast and Fire Judgment on the East Coast will create a Steam Judgment throughout the nation as the aftermath of both will mix together to devastate this country.

It is time to get right with God. It's time to stop playing church and begin to win the lost. There are no amounts of physical preparations that can ready you for what's coming to this country. A frightened unsaved population will scurry to prep for and hoard food, guns, ammo and toilet paper, but God will have a people who are calling for the preparations of the heart.

It is time *"to make ready a people prepared for the Lord."* Prepare your heart...

> *For all this His anger is not turned away, but His hand is stretched out still. For the people do not turn to Him who strikes them, nor do they seek the Lord of Hosts. Therefore the Lord will cut off head and the tail...*
> Isaiah 9:12–14

Who is Worthy?

There are none who are worthy
No not even one
But the Lamb He is coming
In the form of the Son

The book of Revelation is a special writing, as it is a unique introduction into the reality of the resurrected Christ. More than the descriptions of His person which are indescribable, it is a Picasso of his Holiness. This book of Revelation describes more than unimaginable visual scenes of what heaven is like, but it conveys an atmosphere that is experienced at the throne of God, an atmosphere so austere and holy that words cannot do it justice.

After John the Beloved is given the messages to the churches, there begins a description of a "...door standing open in heaven. And the first voice which I heard was like a trumpet speaking with me saying, 'Come up here, and I will show you things which must take place after this'" (Rev. 4:1).

John was no longer hearing that familiar "still small voice" but at this moment he was attuned to a booming, thundering message coming from *"a throne set in heaven, and One sat on the throne"* (vs. 2).

He goes onto describe the One on the throne and its surroundings. It's a magnificent moment in time where John is in the presence of the glorified Jesus who is surrounded by an emerald rainbow encircling the throne. Also, around the throne were twenty-four more thrones with twenty-four elders sitting on those thrones each one clothed in white with crowns of gold on their heads. There was lightning and thunder and voices booming. The reverberating, booming echo of the sounds must have been felt by John to the core of his bones like an unanticipated lions roar in the jungle. He then describes a sea of glass under his feet like beautiful crystal and in the middle of all of this were four living creatures whose description is like something out of a science fiction novel. Each creature was similar in presence and duty with six wings. They are described as having eyes all over their person, the Bible characterizes them as being *"full of eyes around and within"* (vs. 8). Each one is definitely a unique being, as each is said to have a different face: one like a lion, one like a calf, one like a man, and one a flying eagle.

These glorious creatures served one purpose. They do not rest day or night and proclaim, *"Holy, holy, holy, Lord God Almighty, Who was and is and is to come?"* (vs. 8).

Right in the middle of this glorious, holy experience John spotted something in the right hand of Him who sat on the throne. It was a scroll. It had writing on both sides of the parchment and it was sealed up with seven seals. Suddenly he hears a strong angel proclaim this question with a loud voice. *"Who is worthy to open the scroll and to loose its seals?"* (Rev. 5:2).

To each of these inhabitants of heaven but probably primarily to John the angel asks, "Who is worthy?" There is a lot of speculation about who these twenty-four elders are, but nobody really knows. For the sake of argument, let's pretend they are chosen and special from throughout the ages, some of the holiest of all people who have ever walked the earth. Perhaps some of the most respected saints like Noah, Elijah, Enoch. Maybe Peter, Paul, John the Baptist or Polycarp. What of the potential contemporaries like Billy Graham, John Wesley, or David Wilkerson. Whoever these twenty-four elders are, they are deemed unworthy to read the scroll or to even crack the seals thereof. Not even those most holy creatures who's only job is to proclaim "Holy, holy, holy" are worthy to cast their gaze on the message of the scroll or to open its seals.

Upon this epiphany, the epiphany that *"no one in heaven or on the earth or under the earth was able to open the scroll or to look at it"* (vs. 3). John became overwhelmed and began to weep. I can only imagine that it was a very emotional time for him as I am sure it wasn't just a small tear he shed, he seemed overcome with weeping because no one was worthy. Then suddenly in the middle of this agonizing moment for John, one of the elders beckons him to stop weeping for one is found worthy. "...Do not weep. Behold, the Lion of the tribe of Judah, the Root of David has prevailed to open the scroll and to loose its seven seals" (vs. 5). Jesus steps out in all of His glory, a lamb as it had been slain and He came up and took the scroll. As He grasped the judging document in his hand, each of the four magnificent creatures and every one of the twenty-four elders fell at His feet. Then a worship session broke out and all of the inhabitants of heaven began to sing "Worthy is the Lamb."

I fear that we have lost the austere fear and awe of the holiness of God. Prophecy has been relegated to a place of familiarity. Yet the Bible says that no one is worthy to even look upon the contents of that judgment scroll. Jesus is the only one qualified to look on, consume, or convey its message. Today, the body of Christ has fallen into one of two camps. Either we pretend we have some special insight into the future because we have God's ear, or we go to the other extreme and run away from its truth with the excuse that it's too difficult to comprehend.

The fact is Jesus has a message, a prophetic message of warning that He is trying to convey and while He is the only one worthy, the only one with true prophetic insight. He is looking for instruments, everyday people like you and I to breathe His message through, a shofar to blow and to play a special message that will send forth that certain sound of heaven. He is wanting to breathe into the shofar of you and I to a world in desperate need of His message.

The question is, can we hear His breath? Are we an empty vessel? A dead instrument waiting only for the breath-life of God to breathe through us? Jesus wants to breathe a message through the shofar of you. Can you hear Him?

Listen! What do you hear? I hear the tuning of the trumpets in heaven. We have entered the beginning of the end of the end. We are living in a time like no other in history and if you listen intently enough, you can hear the tuning of trumpets in glory. Just as the stage here on earth is being set for the final battle and final judgments, heaven is also preparing to play their part. Prior to every judgment unleashed in the Revelation, a trumpet blast is blown and you can be sure the excitement is mounting in heaven as well as each heavenly creature readies themselves to play their part or blow their trumpet. If you listen intently enough, you will hear the tuning of those trumpets.

As the trumpets are tuned in heaven, there is a reverberation down here on earth. While it is not the "actual" fulfillment of Revelation, I do believe we are experiencing tuning sounds of trumpets in heaven which in turn come in the form of judgments here on earth giving the inhabitants of this planet a glimpse of what is to come. It is one last mercy call to repent and turn to Jesus. He who has an ear to hear, let him hear the tuning of the trumpets in glory.

The Bible expressly states that, "...God does nothing, unless He reveals His secret to His servants the prophets (Amos 3:7). This world is about to undergo a tremendous change through judgment and God wants to warn His people ahead of time as a mercy call to be ready and to have a ready heart. Every judgment that is about to plague mankind can be heard in the tuning of the heavenly trumpets. But you have to put yourself in a place to hear that sound. You have to be willing to receive the message directly from the only One who is worthy...Jesus! Then you must muster the courage to stand and proclaim with the love of Christ the final message to the world that they must turn to Him before it's too late.

But it can't be a message you receive through osmosis from your favorite pastor, preacher, teacher, or prophet and you will not be allowed to plagiarize and declare it as your own just because it sounds good or makes you look like some sort of spiritual giant. The only true message worth proclaiming must come from the only one who is worthy, Jesus Christ.

At the beginning of this chapter, the question was asked, who is worthy? Jesus alone is worthy but, in His estimation, the lost and backslidden are worthy to have a fresh, unadulterated word from heaven. Jesus has a message of life for the lost and it must come through you. The only way to receive that word is spending time with Him. Not five-minute "bless-me" sessions, but intense times of intimacy with Jesus Christ. Spend time in quiet solitude so you can hear His breath sounds. Jesus can say more in one breath than you can read in a volume of books; we just have to be willing to get close enough to Him for Him to want to whisper His secrets.

Sin has separated mankind from the tree of life that was growing in the Garden of Eden and because of that sin, man was driven out of the Edenic garden and God has placed "cherubim at the east of the garden of Eden, and a flaming sword which turned every way, to guard the way to the tree of life" (Gen. 3:24). One day, there will be a reuniting of us with that tree of life (Rev. 22). But until that time, the only access lost mankind has to the life of God comes through Shofar vessels who are yielded to allow God to breathe His breath through them. To a dying man, breath means life and the only chance this world has at the eternal life-breath of God can solely be blown through you or I, the Shofar of God. Hallelujah!

Postponement is Over

No more delaying
*   Postponement is done*
The Liars must stop
*   And My Truth-Sayers come*

Everything contained within the Word of God is true. Every prophetic utterance contained within its pages has either come true already with the first advent of Christ or it is about to come true with the culmination of His second advent. There isn't a Christian on the planet that would dispute the confident statements of that truth.

However, something has crept into the church today very subtly, but glaringly scary. The same attitude that a lost world holds that He is delaying His coming has crept into the church. We have somehow started to believe as the world does that His coming and all of the accompanying events associated with His coming are somehow being delayed. We have come to believe that there is time to defer the decision to follow Christ in holiness and His ways because, well, "There's time." After all, Jesus wouldn't come now. There's still too much to do, too much to experience and surely, He wouldn't come now and disrupt our perfect, prosperous plans for our lives.

The same stall tactic that the world believes in has crept into the body of Christ and we have a deferment mentality when it comes to the end of all things as we know it. Somehow it has crept into our psyche that Jesus has postponed His glorious appearing.

Nothing could be farther from the truth. The framework is being put into place today for the gallows of His saints and yet we will not lay on the cross He has called us to and instead, even though we would not say it openly, we adhere to a world's belief system that His coming has been postponed for a more appropriate time.

God's timing is always perfect and unfortunately, He does not reschedule His appointed times because it's not convenient for us or because our calendar is full. He is coming and this is the beginning of the end of the end.

For I am the Lord, I speak, and the word which I speak will come to pass; it will no more be postponed; for in your days, O rebellious house, I will say the word and perform it, says the Lord God.

Ezekiel 12:25

We are living in a time when God is going to speak and the fulfillment of His words will be instantly fulfilled. He is about to lay to rest the proverb of the people which says, "The days are prolonged, and every vision fails?"(Ez. 12:21) The days of delay to the fulfillment of the prophets words are no longer here. We are living in the day of discharge. God is ready to discharge the proclamations of His prophets.

It is clear that we are living in a time when His people are saying, "The vision that he sees is for many days from now, and he prophesies of times far off" (Ez. 12:27). It is no longer time to believe that prophetic fulfillment has been put on a shelf to be opened at a later date but many of His people don't believe this and instead follow lying tongues to their own destruction.

Why has this happened? Because we have allowed prophets to prophesy out of their own hearts to our destruction and to their prosperity. They have been building ministries on the backs of the poor and plastering their walls with stolen monies. They have lying tongues that relish to get up and coerce the elderly and gullible out of their precious fixed incomes in order to build their walls of plenty. These men and women follow their own spirit and have seen nothing.

> They have envisioned futility and false divination, saying, 'Thus says the Lord!' But the Lord has not sent them yet they hope that the word may be confirmed. Have you not seen a futile vision, and have you not spoken false divination? You say, 'The Lord says,' but I have not spoken. Therefore, thus says the Lord God: "Because you have spoken nonsense and envisioned lies, therefore I am indeed against you," says the Lord God.
>
> Ezekiel 13:6–8

The time of speaking out of your own mind and saying, "Thus says the Lord." is over. God has had enough of this misrepresentation, and if these ministries and "ministers" who rob the poor and direct the lost into dark alleys. If they do not turn from their wicked ways of prophesying out of their own hearts and stop from using nonsensical charms to barter and coerce people out of their inheritances, the only thing that awaits them will be the wrath of the Groom breaking forth to protect His bride.

The time for nonsense soothsaying is over.

*And will you profane Me among My people for
handfuls of barley and for pieces of bread, killing
people who should not die...by your lying to My
people who listen to lies? Therefore thus says the
Lord God: Behold, I am against your magic charms
by which you hunt souls there like birds. I will tear
them from your arms, and let the souls go, the souls
you hung like birds. I will also tear off your veils
and deliver My people out of your hand, and they
shall no longer be as prey in your hand. Then you
shall know that I am the Lord.*

Ezekiel 13:19–21

Instead of reaching the lost and turning them from
their wicked ways, they reach into their pockets to
build their mini-kingdoms, but God has had enough
and those ministries are coming down. He is about to
expose them for what they truly are, liars. The veils are
coming off and God is going to expose them. "Therefore
you shall no longer envision futility nor practice divination; for I will deliver My people out of your hand, and
you shall know that I am the Lord" (Ez. 13:23).

These false prophets have built their fortunes on
the backs of the poor in the body of Christ and the lost
are being kept hostage to their sins. This will not be
allowed any longer. False ministers will fall and their
walls will come down because God is about to expose

them for who they really are. We are about to see what true prophets are supposed to represent and it won't be money, and it won't be fame.

> *My hand will be against the prophets who envision futility and who divine lies; they shall not be in the assembly of My people, nor be written in the record of the house of Israel, nor shall they enter into the land of Israel. Then you shall know that I am the Lord God. Because, indeed, because they have seduced My people, saying, "Peace!" when there is no peace...*
> Ezekiel 13:9–10

The time for postponement, delay, suspension however you want to say it, it is over. True prophets are about to come forth with an instantaneous word of the Lord with fire in their bones and power in their spirits and God will honor their truth by answering with instantaneous fire on the alter. "Therefore say to them, thus says the Lord God: 'None of My words will be postponed any more. But the word which I speak will be done,' says the Lord God" (Ezek. 12:28).

Do You Know Jesus?

I've sensed His presence in the atmosphere
Known He was with me all around
Touching Him so intimately
All I could do was bow to the ground

I've heard Him gently speak to my spirit
His word softly jump from the pages
Imparting knowledge beyond comprehension
Granting wisdom beyond the wisest sages

I've known Him as gracious, loving, and kind
Cleansed by His blood-filled bath
I've been chastened by His white hot tears
Felt the sting of His disciplining wrath

Lamb-Lion of God sitting on His throne
Eyes of fire and robe of white
Ready to split the eastern skies
Judgment day as black as night

Behold He stands in the sky
Once open soon to close is the door
Judgment fire no longer postponed
Jesus clothed King and Lord of Lords

The Shofar—
God's Warning

The Lord He does nothing
Unless to the prophets He shows
Now open up your lungs
And blow Shofar blow

Interlaced throughout the entirety of the Bible is a question that is asked many times with varying answers for the situation. That question is, "Who can but prophesy?" Amos asked these very words. He tells of a message that is spoken to him by the Lord and the corresponding question that comes with the message is, "...The Lord God has spoken! Who can but prophesy?"(Amos 3:8).

The prophetic word is a holy thing and comes with a tremendous responsibility. Many times that message is a warning of things to come and as we approach what I believe is the end of the end, the dispatching word that comes from the throne room is one of impending judgment to a world that has forsaken Him and the question cries out with a resounding gong, *Who can but prophesy?*

> *If a trumpet is blown in a city, will not the people be afraid? If there is calamity in a city, will not the Lord have done it? Surely the Lord does nothing, unless He reveals His secret to His servants the prophets.*
>
> Amos 3:6–7

God has a word that He is speaking but who can but prophesy? I ask that question also because I fear the state of what prophecy has become is far less then what it was meant to be. In many Christian circles, prophecy is either relegated to yesteryear and disdained as not for us today or to the opposite extreme it has become something commonplace.

We have cheapened the prophetic word by making it irrelevant on the one end and common on the other. The prophetic word does not come from a water well that can be drawn at will. It is a Divine Word, spoken from the lips of a glorified Savior, whom the Bible says, He is the only one worthy to break the seals and open the scrolls of impending judgment. If these are truly the last days and the Bible is true, then the prophetic word that will come forth in these last days will be a message of judgment. Yet we are too busy listening to messengers using divination. Messages conjured out of their own hearts and minds masquerading as truth.

Prophecy is holy, but we have made it common. Many think the opposite of holiness is sin but if you think about it, the opposite of holy is common. Prophesy has become the "flavor of the month," ordinary, familiar, and routine, when it is and should be holy, divine, and sacred. "A lion has roared! Who will not fear? The Lord God has spoken! Who can but prophesy?" (Amos 3:8).

It is a holy responsibility to wear the mantle of prophet. Thankfully, Jesus is the mantle bearer and He has a message that must be proclaimed through the sounding of the trumpet(shofar). Become that dead, lifeless piece of antler for God. Be the tusk that His message blows through.

The prophet is God's shofar. Notice that God's word says, "So all this was done that it might be fulfilled which was spoken by the Lord through the prophet... "(Matt. 1:22). Jesus has a prophetic word that He wants to convey to the world and that message is spoken *by the Lord and through the prophet.* We are simply to be the conduit for His breath of life that cascades like water flowing through a faucet.

I know it's difficult to hear or proclaim a word of judgment, but this is the time we are living in. Will you stand with Jesus so the lost and the Church will hear the truth and come to repentance? Will you be brave enough to tell the truth in love?

"Surely the Lord God does nothing, unless He reveals His secret to His servants the prophets" (Amos 3:7). The Bible is clear in this matter. Judgment is on its way and God does nothing until He reveals it to His servants the prophets. This breath of life message can only come through His shofar, you and me.

Lately, I have often asked God, "Why?" Why judge America now? We do so much good in this world! There are so many good people here, why send judgment to America now? God's stated purpose in judgment is very clear, "...Then they shall know that I am the Lord" (Ez. 12:16).

There are voices crying out from the grave that require retribution. God can no longer listen to the screams of babies being murdered in the womb and their corpses used as legal tender, and I stress legal. This nation will be held responsible for not only the murder of millions of innocent babies, but she will also be held responsible for the thousands of children being trafficked for sex and for the racial oppression suffered at the hands of power-hungry authority.

Their deaths cry out from the ground like the murder of Abel did. "The voice of your brother's blood cries out to Me from the ground" (Gen. 4:10). He hears the "outcry" of the innocent being tormented by their captors, rapists, and oppressors. Just as God heard the outcry of Sodom and Gomorrah (Gen. 18:21), He hears the outcry of the innocents being raped and handled like trash. No more! The "outcry" of aborted babies and raped children has been heard in heaven and He is coming down with judgment because we have refused to repent of these abominations against the Lord.

Judgment is here because the time for winking at this travesty is over. Just as God spoke to Abraham and warned Lot before Sodom was destroyed, He is sending his shofar-messengers to sound an alarm. God's message to us is, "For we will destroy this place, because the outcry against them has grown great before the face of the Lord, and the Lord has sent us to destroy it" (Gen. 19:13).

God is about to send Heptad judgment periods upon America followed by Heptad mercy periods. The question is, are you ready?

Heptad Judgment, Mercy, and Revival

Perfection in judgment
   He brings soul survival
Perfection in mercy
   He brings perfect revival

The creation message in Genesis was a Heptad moment. It was a span of time which related to the number seven with extreme significance for the Christian. God created the heavens and the earth and on the seventh day, He rested because He had completed perfectly His masterpiece. That seven-day period was a Heptad moment. A heptad is simply a group or set of seven. It can be days as in Genesis or years as in Daniel's Seventieth Week. In the case of Daniel, he speaks of a Heptad moment in terms of one week or a series of seven that translated for us as the seven-year tribulation period.

In either case, it is a message enshrined in what I call a heptad moment.

America is in the midst of her heptad moment. Not the Great Tribulation that the Bible speaks about. Not a specified amount of time per se, but in God's timetable a moment...a heptad moment which will define her for all eternity.

It is basic common knowledge for a Christian that the number seven signifies "perfection" or "completion." A heptad moment is a period of time determined and sometimes undetermined in length yet perfect and complete in its intent. The Genesis creation was a heptad moment. The Great Tribulation will be a heptad moment, and America is in the midst of her heptad moment.

This moment that we are living in right now is not a prediction of a timeline of judgments for America, though it is.

It is a proclamation that God will execute perfect judgment to bring about appointed results. We are living not only in the last days but the last days of America as we know it. This time is appointed, and it will be a perfect and complete heptad moment designed and orchestrated by God Himself.

America's heptad moment will have many and periodic perfect judgments followed by periods of perfect mercy interlaced with installments of perfect revival.

God's relation to time is different than our relation to time. Although it's difficult to comprehend, the Bible is clear that "...with the Lord one day is as a thousand years, and a thousand years as one day" (2 Pet. 3:8). To God, if a day is as a thousand years, what must a moment be? The timeframe is irrelevant, what is relevant is that we are living in a moment, a heptad moment in time that is appointed by heaven to transform this country in such a complete and perfect way as to stage us into the end time scenario that will bring about the return of the Lord Jesus Christ.

How long will these judgment and mercy periods last? What must we have to endure? Only the prophet Jesus Christ knows. I do know this, it will be perfect, complete, and transformative.

The Egyptian plague judgments in the days of Moses were a heptad moment. It was a period of time whereby God executed perfect judgments interlaced with perfect mercies to bring about an appointed end. Each plague came with increasing intensity and God granted times of mercy in hopes that an opportunity for repentance would bring about transformation for His people.

When mercy failed to bring about God's appointed will, He sent even worse and worse judgments until finally He had to strike the firstborn. (Note: Even this repentance was short-lived and sparked a violent outburst toward God and the people of God but by then, it was too late and Pharaoh's Egyptians were judged with one final torrent right on the cusp of their violent outburst.) I bring this up because it seems violence is the last sign before final judgment falls.

What will you do during America's heptad moment? Habakkuk saw a moment like this during his time. The Bible says, "The burden which the prophet Habakkuk saw" (Hab. 1:1). God had revealed a heptad moment to Habakkuk and what he saw laid upon him such a burden. He saw a people who were "marked for correction" and "appointed...for judgment" and it burdened him. He knew that God could not look on wickedness and the only thing left to bring about transformation was a rod labeled "Heptad Moment."

Habakkuk sensed he was in this moment of time when God was about to do something and his response was, "I will stand my watch and set myself on the rampart (wall) and watch to see what He will say to me..." (Hab. 2:1). Habakkuk's soul was burdened with what was about to happen and though he was anxious about the outcome he waited apprehensively as God's appointed watchman ready to convey God's message.

Then the Lord answered me and said: Write the vision and make it plain on tablets, that he may run who reads it. For the vision is yet for an appointed time, but at the end it will speak, and it will not lie.

51

Though it tarries, wait for it; because it will surely come, it will not tarry.

Habakkuk 2:2–3

The Lord said, "I am about to show you something and I want you to write the vision down even though those who read it will run from it." Habakkuk was faithful and steadfast in his determined response. I ask again, what will you do during America's heptad moment?

Will you be brave enough to proclaim this appointed time, to be that conduit message to bring about repentance? This is an appointed time for America. It does not take a prophet to see that we are living in the same type of consequential vision as Habakkuk. The same judgment that fell then will fall now.

Will not your creditors rise up suddenly? Will they not awaken who oppress you? And you will become their booty. Because you have plundered many nations, all the remnant of the people shall plunder you.

Habakkuk 2:7–8

Just as Habakkuk saw creditors rising up suddenly to oppress and confiscate people's assets as booty, there will be a *foreclosure judgment* that will come upon this

nation as well. We have mortgaged ourselves personally with such a load of debt that the next disaster that
strikes America will cause the "creditors" or financial
institutions to "rise up suddenly" and begin force col-
lections of that debt. Those who cannot pay will lose
their homes and cars and it will happen swiftly as these
institutions will attempt to stop the bleeding, but it will
be to no avail. Secondly, nationally we are saddled with
an even worse debt load that is insurmountable now
and the government will not be able to stem the foreclosure rate, and this will cause people to protest and
riot in desperation.

Habakkuk said "When I heard, my body trembled;
my lips quivered at the voice; rottenness entered my
bones; and I trembled in myself, that I might rest in
the day of trouble..." (Hab. 3:16). I know this is a difficult and scary message. I feel this same trembling that
Habakkuk felt, "But the Lord is in His holy temple, let
all the earth keep silence before Him. For the earth will
be filled with the knowledge of the glory of the Lord..."
(Hab. 2:20, 14).

You and I must center ourselves before the Lord
and proclaim God's message as Habakkuk did and we
will see one of the greatest revivals that has yet to be
experienced. Though there may not be fruit in the gro-
cery basket or meat on the shelf and the job market has
failed and we don't know where the next supply will

come from, yet we must proclaim these words in trust to the Lord. "Yet I will rejoice in the Lord, I will joy in the God of my salvation. The Lord God is my strength; He will make my feet like deer's feet, and He will make me walk on my high hills" (Hab. 3:18–19).

America's heptad moment will be as God's word proclaims it. It will be a moment of judgment, mercy and revival, each in perfect sequence, timing, and intensity, and appointed to bring about God's determined will for this time. "O Lord, I have heard Your speech and was afraid; o Lord, revive your work in the midst of the years! In the midst of the years make it known; In wrath remember mercy" (Hab. 3:2). America's heptad moment, our heptad moment will be perfect judgment interspersed with perfect mercy to bring about perfect revival. God will have His appointed heptad moment.

American Idol Judgments

Prove You are coming
Define for me "soon"
The trumpet is tuning
I hope you have a room

We are living in the last days and as such, I believe we are living in the last days of America. Many people are asking very genuinely and specifically, "What's going to happen next?" The honest answer is only Jesus knows. He is the only one worthy to open the scroll and He is the only one worthy to know the future. However, we have been given very clear direction to discern the signs of the times. The specifics of which we must leave up to Him.

Many asked Jesus this same question.

Then the Pharisees and Sadducees came, and testing Him asked that He would show them a sign from heaven. He answered and said to them, When it is evening you say, It will be fair weather, for the sky is red; and in the morning, It will be foul weather today, for the sky is red and threatening. Hypocrites! You know how to discern the face of the sky, but you cannot discern the signs of the times.

Matthew 16:1–3

In essence, Jesus was saying that you desire specifics to confirm what you already know. That you are living in the midst of the last days and yet live as if He is postponing His arrival for some distant time in the future. As if somehow, He is required to prove His immanency. If ever we should be able to read the signs of the times it should be now. We are in it! It is morning and the sky is red! It only takes a cursory review of the major and minor prophets to see we are quickly approaching the finale. If Elijah lived in our day, he would be making proclamations based off of more than a cloud the size of a man's hand. We are living in a deluge in comparison.

American idol judgments are not on their way, they are here. A quick perusal of the prophets will reveal what God is about to do and what we are in the midst of. How God reacted to nations living in bold and blatant sin in times past is how He will react today to America.

As my hand has found the kingdoms of the idols, whose carved images excelled those of Jerusalem and Samaria, as I have done to Samaria and her idols, shall I not do also to Jerusalem and her idols?

Isaiah 10:10–11

Surely as God has acted in the past He will act in the present and certainly how He is predicted to act in the future judgments of Revelation He will act in the now. American idol judgments are not on their way, they are here.

If God moves against America as He did against the nations living in sin during Isaiah's time, then what awaits us is clear. We have changed from a once humble nation to one with an arrogant heart. We take all the credit and put all of our trust in our own strength and might and all along we are what we are because of Him and not because there is something more virtuous about us than any other people or nation.

God has given us everything we have and yet we take all the credit and glory all of which only belongs to Him.

Therefore it shall come to pass, when the Lord has performed all His work on Mount Zion and on Jerusalem, that He will say, I will punish the fruit of the arrogant heart of the king of Assyria, and the glory of his haughty looks. For he says: By the strength of my hand I have done it, and by my wisdom, for I am prudent...

Isaiah 10:12–13

America is in this same place today that the scripture speaks of. We arrogantly accept the credit for the might of our military strength and the wisdom of our successes. We are in the midst of this same judgment that Isaiah spoke of, "Shall the ax boast itself against him who chops with it? Or shall the saw exalt itself against him who saws with it?...Therefore the Lord, the Lord of hosts, will send leanness among the fat ones" (Is. 10:15–16).

He who has an ear, let him hear what the Spirit says through the prophets of old. The breath of God is cascading through the shofar messengers of the past, but do we hear it? Their message screams at us from the pages of His Holy Word but we are blind through the abstinence of reading it. Hear the Word of the Lord through the vehicle of His Holy Word and minor prophets.

Gather yourselves together, yes, gather together, O undesirable nation before the decree is issued, or the day passes like chaff, before the Lord's fierce anger comes upon you, before the day of the Lord's anger comes upon you!

Zephaniah 2:1–2

For you have said in your heart: "I will ascend into heaven, I will exalt my throne above the stars of God; I will also sit on the mount of the congregation...I will ascend above the heights of the clouds, I will be like the Most High."

Isaiah 14:13, 14

"The day of your watchman and your punishment comes" (Micah 7:4).

"Her priests teach for pay, and her prophets divine for money. Yet they lean on the Lord, and say, Is not the Lord among us? No harm can come upon us" (Micah 3:11).

"Woe to you who desire the day of the Lord! For what good is the day of the Lord to you? It will be darkness, and not light. It will be as though a man fled from a lion, and a bear met him!" (Amos 5:18–19).

Therefore hear this now, you who are given to pleasures, who dwell securely, who say in your heart, I am, and there is no one else besides me; I shall not sit as a widow, nor shall I know the loss of children; But these two things shall come to you in a moment, in one day: The loss of children, and widowhood. They shall come upon you in their fullness because of the multitude of your sorceries, for the great abundance of your enchantments. For you

*have trusted in your wickedness; You have said,
"No one sees me"; Your wisdom and your knowledge have warped you; And you have said in your
heart, "I am, and there is no one else besides me."
Therefore evil shall come upon you; You shall not
know from where it arises. And trouble shall fall
upon you; You will not be able to put it off. And des-
olation shall come upon you suddenly, which you
shall not know.*

Isaiah 47:8–11

"Because your sins have increased, I have done these things to you" (Jer. 30:15).

"All her idols I will lay desolate" (Mal. 1:7).

*A son honors his father, and a servant his master.
If then I am the Father, where is My honor? And if I
am a Master, where is my reverence? Says the Lord
of hosts…But now entreat God's favor, that He may
be gracious to us. While this is being done by your
hands, will He accept you favorably?*

Malachi 1:6, 9

*Hear the word of the Lord! Thus says the Lord God:
"Woe to the foolish prophets, who follow their own
spirit and have seen nothing! They have envisioned
futility and false divination, saying, 'Thus says the*

Lord!' But the Lord has not sent them; yet they hope that the word may be confirmed. Have you not seen a futile vision, and have you not spoken false divination? You say, 'the Lord says,' but I have not spoken." Therefore thus says the Lord God: "Because you have spoken nonsense and envisioned lies, therefore I am indeed against you, Says the Lord God. Because they have seduced My people, saying, Peace! When there is no peace..."

Ezekiel 13:2–3, 6–8, 10

Woe to you who are at ease in Zion. Woe to you who put far off the day of doom, Who lie on beds of ivory, stretch out on your couches, and anoint yourselves with the best ointments, but are not grieved for the affliction of Joseph.

Amos 6:1, 3, 4, 6

Therefore I will judge you...Every one according to his ways, says the Lord God. "Repent, and turn from all your transgressions, so that iniquity will not be your ruin. Cast away from you all the transgressions which you have committed, and get yourselves a new heart and a new spirit. For why should you die? For I have no pleasure in the death of one who dies," Says the Lord God. "Therefore turn and live!"

Ezekiel 18:30–32

The Sound of Repentance

Turn and move forward
Repent of your pride
Stop deceiving yourself
With that moonwalk backslide

Many people misinterpret the true sound of repentance. They wrongfully believe that repentance has to do with an emotional display and sorrowful howling for the things that they've done. Repentance has long carried on its back a stigma of some sort of work performed for salvation. However, the sound of repentance goes well beyond the bounds of emotion and sorrow though they are definitely a part of genuine repentance.

Shame, remorse, contrition all carries with it a definitive sound that accompanies repentance, but true repentance has very little to do with a sound that can be heard and has more to do with something that can be seen. Just as making popcorn in the microwave carries with it a distinct aroma, the aroma itself is not the popcorn; it only enhances that which is coming. True repentance does have a sound but it is an ancillary to the actual.

True repentance is much more than a sound. It is visible, actual, and a necessary element of true Christianity and fellowship with Jesus Christ. Many people get mad when discussing a topic such as repentance, mostly because it is a conversation that requires action, without which we cannot see God. This reaction of anger by many regarding this topic is very understandable and in fact brings a helpful reminder and definition as to what true repentance is.

Repentance requires a change in three things: Mind, Attitude and Direction (MAD). Repentance requires action. There must be a change of mind with regards to sin. A change in attitude about that sin and a moving toward a new direction away from that sin. Without true repentance, the opposite acronym is also true, DAM. You can see why a discussion of this topic brings with it an emotional angst. Repentance requires a drastic change of direction without which we are not allowed access to heaven, resulting in damnation forever.

Therefore I will judge you, O house of Israel, every one according to his ways, says the Lord God. Repent, and turn from all of your transgressions, so that iniquity will not be your ruin. Cast away from you all the transgressions which you have committed, and get yourselves a new heart and a new spirit. For why should you die, O house of Israel? For I have no pleasure in the death of one who dies, says the Lord God. Therefore turn and live!

Ezekiel 18:30–32

It used to go without saying that sin must be abandoned in order to pursue a relationship with Jesus Christ. This old-time religious belief has been hijacked by the liars and false prophets and turned into something obsolete and unrequired. That is a lie from the pit of hell. It is another gospel, but not a pure gospel, no matter how you slice it.

Imagine with me if you will that it is your day of reckoning. Your time on this big blue ball is over and you are about to stand before the throne of almighty God. As you stand there, He asks, "Soul (insert your name), bring before me everything that was most important to you right before I called you before my throne." As you stand there, you reach within your mind's eye for your wife and say, "Here Lord, she was very important to me." God gazes down into your soul as only He can, and you instantly recognize that He feels you are missing something. You search your heart again and say, "Here Lord, my kids and grandkids...they were important to me." Again, just by looking into His eyes you recognize that He knows you are not sharing something that was extremely important to you.

As you search your heart, you cannot fathom what He is wanting and so you ask. "Lord, when I lived my life on the earth, the things that were the most important to me was my relationship with you, my wife, kids, and grandkids."

As you stand there in silence before the throne of God, you begin to tremble. An emotion begins to swell up inside of you that turns into bitterness inside the pit of your stomach as you realize why the throne is silent. As the seconds seem like ages, suddenly He speaks. "Soul, why did you not bring to my throne what was most important to you?"

You say, "What do you mean God?"

"Soul, do you think that I have not seen the life that you have lived in its entirety? There is something you have left out that was more important to you while you were on earth than Me and I want you to go and bring her to Me."

Like a preview in a movie right before your eyes, is a replay of your unrepentant dalliances, God plays them for you in all their inglorious blackness. The porno mistress, the actual mistress, the money mistress, homosexuality mistress, the drunkenness mistress and as they are all displayed, He says, "Bring those things that were most important to you before Me."

"Oh God," you say, "I can't do that. You are so holy and pure, Your brightness overwhelms me and I cannot bring those things into Your presence."

"Soul," He says, "You don't have to bring them, they cling to you like the stench of death. You loved your sins more than Me. Depart from Me you wicked soul into everlasting fire."

That is where we are at this hour. One day, without repentance you will be driven from His presence. The trumpet sound you hear will be one of judgment in all of its declared finality. What is the most important thing in your life today? Wife, family, career, pet sin? The evil and even those good things, if they keep you from giving Him your all, they will keep you from His presence on judgment day.

Go back in time for a moment. Predate all of those good things that have been given to you here on this earth. You are living back in the day when you didn't have any of those things that you so enjoy today. You're single, no kids—only the dream of them—and a longing to have that future family. Suddenly, Satan comes to you in some form promising you the things that you long for in instantaneous fashion. A beautiful wife, two-and-a-half wonderful kids, and prosperity in abundance but he states to you that it will come at a price. In exchange for those good things, you must give your soul. Would you do it? Would you trade your soul to have the wife, job, kids, and stuff that you have today? In a predated existence of those things, you would have never traded your soul to Satan for anything in the world, so why are you trading your soul postdated for those people and things today? "For what profit is it to a man if he gains the whole world, and loses his own soul? Or what will a man give in exchange for his soul?" (Matt. 16:26).

It's not that you can't have those good things. In fact, it is God's greatest desire to bless His children with the desires of their hearts. But those things, those people, those possessions as good and helpful as they are, they cannot take preeminence in your life over God. "For the Son of Man will come in the glory of His Father with His angels, and then He will reward each according to his works" (Matt. 16:27). Repentance is a requirement not only of the despicable things that we are ashamed of, but even the good things that hold supremacy in our hearts. Jesus must be first. "Then Jesus said to His disciples, If anyone desires to come after Me, let him deny himself, and take up his cross and follow Me" (Matt. 16:24).

The sound of repentance is a call and it requires a visible action on the parts of its hearers. It used to be that it was easy to spot a "backslider." They didn't try to hide their sin. They didn't try to justify the life they were living. They just openly struggled with the act of repentance and most of them would even tell you openly. "I'm walking the life of a backslider." Today we no longer backslide, we "moonwalk."

If someone were to cast their gaze in the direction of a moonwalker, they would see a person who looks like he is moving forward but in reality, he's going backwards. It looks fun, in fact it is fun...for a while. While it looks like forward movement is occurring, in fact it is extreme backsliding and even though the crowd continues to cheer. Eventually you have to either stop and turn around or fall off the stage.

The sound of repentance is a summoning against sin. A call to war. As Christians, we look forward to a promised day when Jesus will return with His army of angels and saints and repentance is a call to that war; a trumpet blast to ride with Him against the master of a sinful race. "And the armies in heaven, clothed in fine linen, white and clean, followed Him on white horses" (Rev. 19:14). Make no mistake. To be one of the armies spoken of in the book of Revelation as following the king on white horses to earth, you must first follow Him on earth.

If you listen, you can hear the trumpet sound and the call to repentance. It is His last call to you. Hurry before it's too late. Turn to Him and live. God always gives a final call to the people of God to come out and journey with Him before judgment falls and that call is going out today. Judgment is about to fall so you must hurry up and relocate.

This same call went out to Noah before the flood. He was called to relocate to the Ark before judgment fell. The same call went out to Lot and his family before judgment fell on Sodom and Gomorrah. The Bible says, "Then the men said to Lot, "Have you anyone else here? Son-in-law, your sons, your daughters, and whomever you have in the city—take them out of this place! For we will destroy this place. When the morning dawned, the angels urged Lot to hurry, saying, "Arise, take your wife and your two daughters who are here, lest you be consumed in the punishment of the city. Hurry, escape there. For I cannot do anything until you arrive there." Then the Lord rained brimstone and fire on Sodom and Gomorrah, from the Lord out of the heavens." (Gen. 19:12–13,15, 22,24).

The sound of repentance is the sound of relocation at heaven's behest. It is time to relocate from sin to Jesus. Sin and soul ties must be cast aside in repentance if we are to survive what is on the horizon. Judgment is coming and we must be on the right side of the rope during this tug-of-war.

You see repentance is not a one-time act. It is a continuous activity and reaction to sin. It is a constant tug of war with sin, the world, and the devil. It is as if there is a giant rope extended from earth to heaven and that rope is being pulled by both sides. On one side is the world and Satan. Anchoring their side of the rope is the immoveable object we call sin. On the other side of the rope is all of heaven: angels, saints, and the unstoppable force of God Himself.

Sinner, devil and demons pulling for all their worth on one side and saints and angels on the other heaving the opposite direction anchored by Jesus Christ. As this tug of war continues, you will be and are being asked to choose a side to pull from. Dig your heels in, chalk your hands, and grab the rope. Make no mistake, one day the rope being pulled by the immoveable object and the unstoppable force will suddenly break. When that rope snaps, the pull will be over and sin, sinner, devil, and demons will be flung to the ground in exhausted desperation with an instant realization that they have just lost the war. When that rope unravels and breaks the pull will be over for the saints as well only they will be catapulted into the heavens as God's word declares,

*For the Lord Himself will descend from heaven
with a shout, with the voice of an archangel, and
with the trumpet of God. And the dead in Christ
will rise first. Then we who are alive and remain
shall be caught up together with them in the clouds
to meet the Lord in the air. And thus we shall always be with the Lord.*

1 Thessalonians 4:16–17

"Let no one deceive you by any means; for that Day
will not come unless the falling away comes first..." (2
Thess. 2:3).

Judgments during this time of tug-of-war are literally God saying to the world, "Let My people go!" and
then one day, "Snap," that rope will break and glory to
God, *rapture!*

Before it's too late, the sound of repentance is a call
to relocate. To relocate from sin to Jesus. Judgment is
here and the only respite is Jesus Christ. Jesus is coming
one day to rapture His bride from this earth but until
that day, the Bible is very clear that the degradation on
this planet will get worse and worse. Relocate into His
presence and cast your sin at His feet. When confront-
ed with sin the natural man screams silently, "Where
will we go?" The Spirit of God says go to Goshen.

Do you remember the story of Joseph? He was Ja-
cob's eleventh son whom he loved dearly but Josephs

brothers hated him because of their jealousy for their fathers love for Joseph. Joseph was betrayed by his brothers and sold into slavery. Every Bible scholar says that Joseph is one of the purest types of Christ in the Old Testament. There are so many parallels of his life to the life of Christ that it boggles the mind, but it serves to teach us something about Jesus.

On the day of reconciliation when Joseph was re-united with his family. He told his brothers to:

> *Hurry and go up to my father, and say to him, Thus says your son Joseph; God has made me lord of all Egypt; come down to me, do not tarry. You shall dwell in the land of Goshen...There I will pro-vide for you lest you and your household, and all that you have come to poverty.*
>
> Genesis 45:9–11

You see, Joseph had interpreted a prophetic dream for Pharaoh and they were in the midst of a famine, much like the United States shall soon be in and Joseph tells the ones that he loves to come and dwell in Goshen so that he can provide for them during this terrible time.

Joseph is a type of Christ and just as Joseph was call-ing to his beloved to come to Goshen so that he can provide for them during this time of famine, even so,

Jesus is calling us to come to Goshen so that He too can provide for us during this time so that we do not come to poverty.

What is the significance of Goshen? Why did Joseph need for his family to go there? Goshen means, "drawing near" (1657 Strongs). You see the significance wasn't in the place of Goshen; it was in the call to draw near to Joseph. Jesus is calling us to draw near to Him even as Joseph called his family to Goshen that He might provide for them, that they might not go into poverty during this terrible time.

Remember who Jesus fed! He didn't feed everybody in the cities where He was located. He fed the 5,000 who drew near to Him. At the last supper, He fed the twelve who came near to Him. Even after His resurrection, He fed Peter when he drew near to Him on the beach. You see Jesus provides for those who draw near to Him. Please, please, please draw near to Him before it's too late so that He can show you His tender care and mercy.

Consummation Judgments

Blinded love making
Intercourse with your sin
She is your debauchery
Your laws the masculine

There is one thing that my Dad instilled in me as a child and that was an intense sense of patriotism. I love the United States of America. I feel blessed everyday just to call myself an American. This country is viewed by everyone, even those who hate us as the greatest Empire ever. There is none to compare throughout the annuls of time. As such, it has been difficult for me to understand why God would judge her so. I have wrestled within myself and with God over the "Why?" of it all.

As He began to scrape the scales from my eyes, I had a deep sense of agony, and still do for this nation. Even now, sometimes I forget and continue to question, but He gently reminds me of His great love for this country as well and He cannot leave us in the state that we are in because the tug-of-war rope is unraveling and about to break, and as such He must hurry to bring to repentance as many as possible before it's too late.

While His great love for us is the reason He must act, He must also act because of our great sin that has been consummated. The events that are about to unfold will impact each of us personally and nationally. It will be felt by unbelievers and believers alike. Most will refuse to hear but there will be a remnant that will turn and live.

No one can deny that not only have we forsaken Him, but it doesn't take long to recognize that we are living in the time and place that Isaiah spoke of when he said, "Woe to those who call evil good, and good evil..." (Is. 5:20). We live in a time when our sin has been consummated and judgment must fall.

Consummation is an act of a feminine and masculine combining as one. It is the act of making a marriage or relationship complete by having intercourse, by which completing the transaction of two becoming one. It is an act of finality and completion, the culmination of a lifelong commitment to stay together "until death do us part."

Consummation of sin takes two parties as well and if "sin activity" is the feminine and "legislation" is the masculine and the two coming together is a protected act, then consummation has occurred. You see, sin on its own does not necessarily bring judgment or chastisement. But when sin is protected, legislated, and violently sheltered, the act of consummation has occurred, and God must act. This nation has moved past her sin and has consummated it with defiant acts of legislation, protecting her and safeguarding her rights. In doing so, there is only one thing that can separate the two.

Even in the Christian life, there is a difference. If you are an honest soul, you have to admit that as true blue as you try to walk in the spirit there are times when sin overtakes you. Yet, God doesn't judge you. Why? Because there is a difference between committing sin and being committed to sin. Nobody will be judged in this life over his struggles with sin. Judgment or chastisements come when "committing sin" changes to being "committed to sin." The moment a person opposes the truth and protects, hides, and hypocritically masquerades his sin, that is the moment judgment/chastisement must occur for that sin.

It's true personally and it's true nationally. We are not only a nation that has committed acts of abortion, we are a nation that has legislated abortion. We have gone from committing the act of murder to authoriz-

We are all slaves to Sin until we are saved.

ing it and even worse at times financing it. The sin of murder has been consummated in the United States of America.

It used to be that homosexuality was a hidden sin committed only by a few and today it has been promulgated by media, Hollywood, and our government officials. Many states have legalized an act that the Bible says is unnatural and as such it has become a national sin that has been consummated by its legalization.

Mind-altering substances have gone beyond the casual act of partaking of a few libations. It has now become the norm to see a billboard on the highway of a marijuana leaf with the statement which reads "Don't Drive Buzzed."

Not only has consummation occurred with regards to these few sinful acts mentioned but take any of those things away and it would be violently opposed by the people. Consummation of the sin of homosexuality, sorcery (drugs), and murder has taken place by and in our nation. The consummation transaction that commits the two together for life has occurred and as such there is only one thing that will twain the two apart.

Lastly, we have become a nation that has sinned by her self-sufficiency. We no longer have a need for God. As He reaches out to help, we push Him away and He must lift His hand. As He removes His hand that is reaching down to help, we are pushing away His hand of divine protection. We have forsaken Him and as such He does not stay where He is not wanted. There were many a time in the gospels when Jesus left places and people when He was not wanted. When He is not wanted by independently-spirited people, He will leave them in their self-sufficiency. The same with a nation.

The sin of this nation (feminine) and the decreed protection of her by the government of the people (masculine) has been consummated. We are now at the point at which our commitment to these sins of anathema have been stamped with the final authoritative approval by the covering of intercourse of legislated protection. God must act in mercy fulminating in judgment. "Woe to you who fulminate anathemas which cannot be reversed" (Enoch 95:4).

The United States of America has made a transaction for life by consummation through the legislation of sin. We have reached the apex of God seeing as He did in the days of Noah. "Then the Lord saw that the wickedness of man was great in the earth, and that every intent of the thoughts of his heart was only evil continually" (Gen. 6:5). God have mercy as we continue to refuse to hear the sounding call of repentance and begin to experience the consummation judgments that are upon us.

Enoch's Last Days' Message

Translated to the heavens
 His holiness I perceived
Seized me by my hand
 All His secrets to show me
Head of Days so frightening
 White as wool and pure as snow
The Most High with His angels
 His whole being seemed to glow
Run away, run away
 A commotion deep inside
The Holy Great One, purest of all
 Jesus Christ The Most High

Recently I have a renewed interest in a parchment written long ago, the book of Enoch. While the book of Enoch is not recognized as a part of the canon of scripture, it is broadly documented as an amazing supplement to scripture. The first century Christians held it in high regard and read it often and it is even a work that is quoted in scripture numerous times.

The writers of Enoch, and I say writers because from a cursory reading it appears to be written by several different authors passed down from generation to generation. Whether written by Enoch, Noah, or Methuselah there is regardless a message to this "Last Days" generation from the namesake of this book that should not be overlooked.

The Bible says of Enoch, "And Enoch walked with God; and he was not, for God took him" (Gen. 5:24). The book of Enoch is partly a depiction of the life and experiences of Enoch. It is a fragmented account of what happened next or during Enoch's lifetime along with other documented warnings and historical accounts of his life and the life of his family. Besides being an intriguing and wonderful read, within the pages of this small little book is a message from Enoch. It is a prophetic message passed down to Noah and his family regarding the flood judgment and the details of that period, but there is also a message to this Last Days Generation. *but not a canonical message*

I have often wondered about Enoch and what became of him. The supplemental reading of this book gives an account of that day when God took him.

And it came to pass after this that his name during his lifetime was raised aloft to that Son of Man and to the Lord of Spirits from amongst those who dwell on the earth. And he was raised aloft on the chariots of the spirit and his name vanished among them.

Enoch 70:1–2

The very next chapter is reminiscent of John the Revelator's writings.

And it came to pass after this that my spirit was translated and it ascended into the heavens; and I saw the holy sons of God. They were stepping on flames of fire; their garments were white (and their raiment), and their faces shone like snow. And I saw two streams of fire, and the light of that fire shone like hyacinth, and I fell on my face before the Lord of Spirits. And the angel Michael (one of the archangels) seized me by my right hand, and lifted me up and led me forth into all of the secrets, and he showed me all the secrets of righteousness. And he showed all the secrets of the ends of the heaven and all the chambers of all the stars and all the luminaries, whence they proceed before the face of the holy ones.

And he translated my spirit into the heaven of heavens, and I saw there as it were a structure built of crystals, and between those crystals tongues of living fire. And my spirit saw the girdle which girt that house of fire, and on its four sides were streams full of living fire, and they girt that house.

And round about were Seraphin, Cherubic, and Ophannin: And these are they who sleep not and guard the throne of His glory. And I saw angels who could not be counted, A thousand thousands, and ten thousand times ten thousand, encircling that house. And Michael, and Raphael, and Gabriel, and Phanuel, and the holy angels who are above the heavens, go in and out of that house. And they came forth from that house, and Michael and Gabriel, Raphael and Phanuel, and many holy angels without number. And with them the Head of Days, His head white and pure as wool, and His raiment indescribable. And I fell on my face, and my whole body became relaxed, and my spirit was transfigured; and I cried with a loud voice...with the spirit of power, and blessed and glorified and extolled. And these blessings which went forth out of my mouth were well pleasing before that Head of Days.

And that Head of Days came with Michael and Gabriel, Raphael and Phanuel, thousands and ten thousands of angels without number. And he (the angel) came to me and greeted me with His voice, and said unto me: This is the Son of Man who is born unto righteousness; and righteousness abides over him, and the righteousness of the Head of Days forsakes him not.

the son of Man needs no introduction!

Enoch 71:1–14

Enoch seems to be the first of a handful of men who have been allowed a glimpse of the Son of Man and Head of Days in all of His glorified existence. He was also given a glimpse of judgment day and several judgments to come and most of it shook him to the core of his being. He said, "Then I wept with a great weeping and my tears stayed not till I could no longer endure it: when I saw, they flowed on account of what I had seen; for everything shall come and be fulfilled..." (Enoch 90:41).

Enoch too was a man just like you and I and as he experienced the righteous glory of the Son of Man; he was stricken by His other worldliness. It was indescribable and incomprehensible and the magnitude of where he came from and who he was, overwhelmed him in the presence of such greatness. Couple that with the vision of judgment to come and he wept a great weeping.

Enoch passed on this message to his family that everything must happen as heaven has proclaimed it to be.

> *For the word calls me, and the spirit is poured out upon me, that I may show you everything that shall befall you forever...and draw not nigh to uprightness with a double heart, and associate not with those of a double heart, but walk in righteousness...and it shall guide you on good paths...For I know that violence must increase on the earth, and great chastisement be executed on the earth, and all unrighteousness come to an end: Yea, it shall be cut off from its roots, and its whole structure be destroyed.*

Enoch 91:1, 4–5

I believe this was a warning of the flood judgment that was to come upon Noah's generation. This writing was Enoch's attempt to pass it on from generation to generation. This vision that Enoch conveyed saved his remnant family and not only continued his personal lineage, but it also preserved the national and spiritual lineage as well. Only Noah & his family were saved, not his brother and sisters

Enoch once again has a message he has tried to convey in this writing. It is his attempt to warn a Last Days

Remnant to come. Here is the vision and the corresponding message for the Last Day Sinner from Enoch.

I saw how a mighty quaking made the heaven of heavens to quake, and the host of the Most High, and the angels, a thousand thousands and ten thousands times ten thousand, were disquieted with a great disquiet. And the Head of Days sat on the throne of His glory, and the angels and the righteous stood around Him. And a great trembling seized me, and fear took hold of me, and my loins gave way, and dissolved were my reins, and I fell on my face. And Michael sent another angel from among the holy ones and he raised me up, and when he had raised me up my spirit returned; for I had not been able to endure the look of the host, and the commotion and the quaking of the heaven. And Michael said unto me: Why art thou disquieted with such a vision? Until this day lasted the day of His mercy; and he hath been merciful and long-suffering towards those who dwell on the earth. And when the day, and the power, and the punishment, and the judgement come, which the Lord of Spirits hath prepared for those who worship not the righteous law, and for those who deny the righteous judgement, and for those who take His name in vain-that day is prepared, for the elect a covenant, but for sinners an inquisition. When the punishment of the Lord of Spirits shall rest upon them, it shall rest in order that the punishment of the Lord of Spirits may not come, in vain... Afterwards the judgement shall take place according to His mercy and His patience.

Enoch 60:1–6

Woe to you who acquire silver and gold in unrighteousness and say: We have become rich with riches and have possessions; and have acquired everything we have desired...For your riches shall not abide but speedily ascend from you; for ye have acquired it all in unrighteousness, and ye shall be given over to a great curse. I have sworn unto you, ye sinners, as a mountain has not become a slave, and a hill does not become the handmaid of a woman, even so sin has not been sent upon the earth, but man of himself has created it, and under a great curse shall they fall who commit it. I have sworn unto you, ye sinners, by the Holy Great One, that all your evil deeds are revealed in the heavens, and that none of your deeds of oppression are covered or hidden. And do not think in your spirit nor say in your heart that ye do not know and that ye do not see that every sin is every day recorded in heaven in the presence of the Most High. And now, know ye that ye are prepared for the day of destruction: wherefore do not hope to live, ye sinners, but ye shall depart and die; for ye know no ransom; for ye are prepared for the day of the great judgment, for the day of tribulation and great shame for your spirits. Woe to you, ye obstinate of heart.

Enoch 97:8, 10; 98:4, 6–7, 10–11

The words of Enoch speak for themselves but a critical message for all of us to take heart is this: when His judgment finally comes, and it is here, it is here because, "Until this day lasted the day of His mercy; and he hath been merciful and long-suffering towards those who dwell on the earth."

this chapter should not be included!

The Mystery of Babylon's Final Hour

Mystery, Babylon Mystery
Your secret difficult to perceive
Your final hour has finally come
The great whore of the great sea

It's quite curious that of all the nations mentioned in the Bible, America is not one of them. She is oddly absent from the annuls of scripture. Why? In the end time scenarios that seem to be playing out right before our very eyes, many nations are mentioned very clearly. You can see Russia's role in the end time predictions. You can see Iran's role in the prophetic lens. Crystal clear is Europe and the revised Roman Empire that is to come. Even China or the kings of the East are represented at the conclusion of the end time scenario. Why not the United States of America? Especially given that there has never been a nation as powerful, with as much influence or affluence. No nation has ever had as many resources as she has.

Since the birth of the United States of America she has been from cradle to adulthood the greatest nation story ever told and yet oddly, she is absent from the end time scenario in the Bible. Or is she?

The Bible speaks of a "Mystery, Babylon the great..." (Rev. 17:5). It says of her that she is a great city. A harlot city that carries with her a mystery identity. The very term mystery implies that it is something as yet un-revealed. A secret if you will and yet something to be sought out or solved. A hidden nugget to be discovered or found. Not something un-knowable but something that can be known through searching the scriptures and receiving enlightenment from the revelatory Spirit of God.

Could it be that America isn't absent from scripture at all but that she is just tucked away inside what the Bible calls this mystery?

The book of Revelation clearly speaks of a Babylon and yet on October 12, 539 BC, Babylon fell to Cyrus of Persia and from that point on, the decay of that city began and to this day, Babylon has never truly been re-vived in all of her predicted glory. (Ref. Ungers pg. 386)

With that being the case, is this Mystery Babylon that the Bible speaks of literal, figurative, metaphorical, allegorical, or symbolic? Is it possible that there are divergent meanings and instead of pigeonholing the meaning into one strict interpretation could there possibly be multiple directions to go and yet keep its intended meaning intact?

Many adhere to a strict interpretation from an "all-knowing" perspective, but could this refer to both an ecclesiastical-geopolitical future harlot and simultaneously be both literal and figurative in the present as represented by the United States of America?

You see, we tend to interpret scripture as linear and yet most of scripture with regards to the first Advent of Christ did not occur in a linear fashion. It happened perfectly as prophesied but certainly not in a linear timeline obviously spelled out. On the contrary, it was mostly curvilinear and divergent. Christ's first coming was not something elementarily predicted; it had to be extrapolated from various points throughout scripture. His first coming while very clear throughout scripture, was never given on a linear plane. *I'm lost*

We would like to imagine Christ's second coming as ultra-predictable and linear in nature, especially given the apparent linear nature of the book of Revelation. I suspect quite the opposite is true. He will come the second time just as He has said, but He will come as a thief in the night with signs apparent but scarcely linear. I suspect His coming will be just as He spoke, and it will come as a shock to most and yet it will adhere to scripture predictions perfectly. IT MUST !

If America is not the Harlot City forecasted in this end-time scenario, she will certainly be an example or type to look back on by the literal and future Mystery Babylon of what to expect when the revised Roman Empire rises to power.

Jeremiah, when speaking of the destruction of Babylon, says that a nation will come from the North, bringing with it the same destructive power that Sodom and Gomorrah experienced and that from the aftermath of that great burning a new set of nations will arise. "Behold, a people shall come from the north, and a great nation and many kings shall be raised up from the ends of the earth" (Jer. 50:41). I believe this scripture speaks of the destruction of Babylon being the catalyst of raising a "many kings" conglomeration of nations; could this be the revised Roman Empire?

Is the United States the whore of Babylon the Bible speaks about? I don't know, but what I do know is there are enough similarities that we will receive at some point and not in measure, the fullness of her judgments.

Let's look at some similarities. "Then one of the seven angels who had the seven bowls came and talked with me, saying to me, 'Come, I will show you the judgment of the great harlot who sits on many waters,'" (Rev. 17:1). The Bible does a great job of interpreting itself much of the time and in this instance does so beautifully. "Then he said to me, The waters which you saw, where the harlot sits, are peoples, multitudes, nations, and tongues" (Rev. 17:15). What nation ever in the history of mankind can boast of being a "melting-pot" of nationalities, peoples, and languages. If you go to Italy who do you find? Italians. If you go to Russia who do you find? Russians. If you go to America who do you find? You find people from every tongue, tribe, and race from all over the world. No other country can boast such a spectacular divergency of people, except of course Babylon the Great.

We are a nation of capitalism, merchandisers of all sorts. The United States commerce of buying and selling is the fountainhead of prosperity for the entire planet. No other nation can make that boast. Yet, when Babylon is destroyed the Bible says of her,

> And the merchants of the earth will weep and mourn over her for no one buys their merchandise anymore: merchandise of gold and silver, precious stones and pearls, fine linen and purple, silk and scarlet, every kind of object...fragrant oil...iron... wheat, cattle, and sheep...and chariots.
>
> Revelation 18:11–13

No other nation can boast of a commerce system as the United States of America except of course, Babylon the Great in the book of Revelation.

Don't be surprised if when we get to heaven, we hear the same thing regarding Babylon the Great that Jesus said to the multitude about John the Baptist and Elijah. You see, everyone was anticipating that before the Messiah would come that Elijah would first come as the forerunner. Jesus said of John the Baptist, "Behold, I send My messenger before Your face, who will prepare Your way before You. And if you are willing to receive it, he is Elijah who is to come" (Matt. 11:10, 14). I will not be surprised if when many get to heaven and they ask, "But Lord, I thought Babylon the Great must first rise and be destroyed before your Second Coming?" And Jesus replies, "Behold, if you are willing to receive it, the United States is Babylon the Great."

You see, according to scripture, Elijah existed in the Old Testament and God took him up in a whirlwind. Elijah has come as prophetically proclaimed. At the First Coming of Jesus, they believed Elijah was coming first and he did come in the person of John the Baptist. At the second coming, many believe Elijah will again be the forerunner to Jesus' return. This is a diverse or curvilinear understanding of scripture which may also be true in this instance with regards to Babylon the Great and the United States of America.

93

I believe Elijah is one of the 2 witnesses of Rev 11

Regardless of your personal interpretation whether literal, figurative, or allegorical. The outcome is the same. "And another angel followed, saying, 'Babylon is fallen, is fallen, that great city, because she has made all nations drink of the wine of the wrath of her fornication'" (Rev. 14:8).

Are we living in the times of the book of Revelation? No, but we are living in the time that is the catalyst for the events of the book of Revelation.

Jeremiah the prophet and John the Beloved both prophesy devastating judgments to come, which I believe perfectly explain what we can expect and why we do not recognize the United States in scripture. Because she exists as the Harlot City, Babylon the Great:

- **Sudden and Catastrophic.**

   Most will be unaware and blind to the impending judgment that is to befall this nation. It will be an unexpected shock to the whole world. "You have indeed been trapped, O Babylon, and you were not aware; You have been found and also caught, because you have contended against the Lord" (Jer. 50:24). "...Alas, alas, that great city Babylon, that mighty city! For in one hour your judgment has come" (Rev. 18:10).

- **It will come from the North.**

  "For out of the north a nation comes up against her, which will make her desolate..." (Jer. 50:3). What superpower who lives in the North with nuclear capability could exact such a strike? Is this a warning of Russia's sneak attack upon the United States?

- **It will be nuclear devastation.**

  "As God overthrew Sodom and Gomorrah and their neighbors, says the Lord, so no one shall reside there, nor son of man dwell in it" (Jer. 50:40). "In the measure that she glorified herself and lived luxuriously in the same measure give her torment and sorrow; for she says in her heart, 'I sit as queen, and am no widow and will not see sorrow.' Therefore her plagues will come in one day-death and mourning and famine. And she will be utterly burned with fire, for strong is the Lord God who judges her" (Rev. 18:7–8).

- **There will be nuclear fall-out.**

  "Because of the wrath of the Lord, she shall not be inhabited, but she shall be wholly desolate. Everyone who goes by Babylon shall be horrified and hiss at all her plagues" (Jer. 50:13). "The kings of the earth who committed fornication and lived luxuriously with her will weep and lament for her, when they see the smoke of her burning, standing at a distance for fear of her torment..." (Rev. 18:9–10).

- **There will be a precursor of a Great Depression, chaos, and rioting.**
  "Therefore her young men shall fall in the streets... I will kindle a fire in his cities, and it will devour all around them." (Jer. 50:30,32). "For in one hour such great riches came to nothing" (Rev. 18:17).

- **It will come with brutal finality.**
  "...It shall be inhabited no more forever, nor shall it be dwelt in from generation to generation" (Jer. 50:39). "And I cried out when they saw the smoke of her burning, saying, what is like this great city...For in one hour she is made desolate" (Rev. 18:18–19).

Is there hope for America? I don't know, but there is hope for Americans! It is time for us to answer the voice from heaven.

And I heard another voice from heaven saying, Come out of her, my people, lest you share in her sins, and lest you receive of her plagues. For her

remember, this is the tribulation period — we are not part of the tribulation

sins have reached to heaven, and God has remembered her iniquities.

Revelation 18:4–5

This is not a call to leave the country, this is a call to come out of her sins. It is time to repent not only for our personal sins but for the sins of this nation. There is a window of opportunity, but I sense it is a window of rescue not one of respite.

There is no time left. Postponement is no longer an option. Come out of her before it's too late. Don't stand before the throne and say, "I thought (this) would happen first," only to hear Him say, "Even as Elijah has come as represented by John the Baptist, even so Babylon the Great has already come represented by the United States of America."

Empirical Change

She basks in her magnificence
    Bathes in Self-Sufficiency
I fear she fails to recognize
    The absence of all of Me

Whenever a nation becomes so enamored with herself that her pride and arrogance take over, she begins to proclaim her magnificence and in doing so, rejects the One who established her for her intended purposes. She begins to assume that she will always be on a destined course for greatness and any calamity can be overcome or rebuilt by her confident assertion of *self-sufficiency.*

What she fails to recognize or remember is that God ordained her path with not only Him as the mastermind but also as the originator, protector, and sustainer of that dream because He is not only a "part" of it, He is the "whole" of it.

By her independence, she removes Him from the equation and she utterly destroys and changes her inheritance and destiny by being the catalyst that provokes Him into lifting His hand of protection and all she has left to declare is, "...We are utterly destroyed! He has changed the heritage of my people; How He has removed it from me!" (Micah 2:4). At some point, if she begins to believe that the promised legacy was a birthright, an entitlement that cannot be removed or changed, then He must alter the trajectory of that nation toward an empirical change.

We often boast that the United States was founded on God and she was, but if that is so, then where is His Honor? If God is the "Founding Father" of America then, "A son honors his father, and a servant his master, if then I am the Father, where is my honor? And if I am a Master, where is My reverence?" (Mal. 1:6). If He truly founded this nation, then why have we removed our honor for Him and reverence from Him?

Is He honored when we remove every vestige of Him from our courtrooms by allowing the Ten Commandments to be removed? Is He revered when we remove prayer from our schools? Is He esteemed when He is used as a "catchphrase" at the end of a presidential message which says, "...and God bless America"? Will He be respected and valued when we allow Him to be removed from our currency? "Because My people have forgotten Me, they have burned incense to worthless idols (the idol of self-sufficiency) and they have caused themselves to stumble in their ways, from the ancient paths..." (Jer. 18:15, *clarification mine*).

If I am not being forthright enough, let me spell it out loud and clear. God is saying to us, "America, if I have fathered this nation, where is my honor?"

On a moral scale, America is in a fast decline. In fact, she has been sick for a very long time and near death. She doesn't recognize it because it has occurred gradually over time and hospice care has been kind to her. It has not been a single sudden ailment that has brought her to this point, but a gradual slide into a weak and afflicted state. She has been rubbed or worn over time like an old shoe into an infirm state of immoral descent.

"In those days Hezekiah was sick, and near death" (2 Kings 20:1a). Like Hezekiah in his time, the United States too is sick and near death, but God in His mercy is offering a window of opportunity. We'll call that opportunity the Window of Hezekiah. God is sending out prophets just as He sent Isaiah to Hezekiah with that same message. "...And Isaiah the prophet, the son of Amoz, went to him and said to him, Thus says the Lord: Set your house in order for you shall die, and not live" (2 Kings 20:1b).

There are many messengers of God who are now or will be proclaiming a word of exactitude judgment to

too many analogies

this sick and dying nation in hopes that it will provoke her to humility and repentance.

When Hezekiah was given this awful message of his halted life, it brought him to his knees. The Bible says he, "…turned his face toward the wall, and prayed to the Lord" (2 Kings 20:2). Hezekiah came to the Lord and he didn't make excuses. In fact, he said in his prayer, "What shall I say? He has both spoken to me, and He Himself has done it" (Isa. 38:15).

And yet even knowing this determined end was established by the Lord Himself which was declared by the prophet Isaiah, Hezekiah went to prayer and reasoned with the Lord and with many words and in repentance he cried out, "For Sheol cannot thank You, death cannot praise You; Those who go down to the pit cannot hope for your truth. The living, the living man, he shall praise You. As I do this day" (Isa. 38:18–19). He pleaded with God that only a living man can praise You and honor You. Once I am dead I cannot praise you from there. He begged for more time to proof out a life worth living and asking for a second chance and God gave him an additional 15-years to live and to live up to what he promised of his life.

"I have heard your prayer, I have seen your tears; surely I will heal you…and I will add to your days fifteen years…for My own sake" (2Kings 20:5,6). God is offering this same window of opportunity to America. There is a

not directly by scripture

pronouncement of sickness and death being held over her proverbial head. Looking for her to humble herself and cast herself at His feet for strength. The body of Christ must become this voice of Isaiah the prophet to America declaring this bitter appointment with death in hopes that she will be granted a Hezekiah window of time.

The United States of America has a limited time to respond to this call as she is already under His awful hand of judgment. During this time, God is granting periods of mercy with infusions of blessings in order to bring about repentance throughout His progressive judgments.

There have been many interpretations of the recent four blood moons, much of which has been with creative license. However, while I am sure there is a theological message difficult to be extrapolated and understood, I firmly believe it is much simpler than that. The four blood moons is a "time-marker" from God to the world. Certainly, there is a message for the church and certainly there is a message for Israel. The bigger picture message is from God for the whole world.

From 2015 on, the global dynamics have undergone a seismic change in order to set the stage for the end of the end and the evil one. It is a time for the hastening of events in order to bring about the fulfillment of scripture for the final One World government, currency, re-

Used by John Haggee

ligion, and Mark of the Beast. The antichrist is about to burst onto the scene, and he will come amidst chaos and war and attempt to establish his final stand against Christ and set himself up to be worshiped as god by all peoples.

The next few years for the United States will be interspersed with hammer strikes of judgment with reprieves of mercy to allow for repentance. This is His final call and at the end of this time, there will come a final economic blow catapulting America into a deep, dark, irreversible economic Hyper-Depression that will last until the Hezekiah Window closes. During this time, not only will she be weak financially, she will be helpless globally and will experience violence internally with civil unrest and riotous chaos.

If national repentance hasn't occurred during this Hezekiah Window of time, America will be brought down with fire and nuclear devastation while she is in this weakened state. She will be helpless to defend herself which will bring about an empirical change with fighting within and without. This is America's last chance; it is her Hezekiah Window.

Even as Hezekiah asked for a sign as proof for this message from the Almighty through the Shofar of Isaiah, so today there is a sign that the Bible gives us to know that this time is drawing near. The final sign before final judgment is clear throughout God's word. The final sign before judgment is violence.

Habakkuk said, "O Lord, how long shall I cry...even cry out to you, Violence!" Habakkuk, as he stood upon the rampart, cried out to God, literally screaming for His attention to see the violence taking place and pleading for Him to put a stop to it.

Jeremiah also saw a day coming upon which would be terrible violence throughout the land and he proclaimed coming judgment "...And violence in the land, ruler against ruler, Therefore behold, the days are coming that I will bring judgment..." (Jer. 51:46–47). Lastly, as in the days of Noah so in our day, "The earth also was corrupt before God, and the earth was filled with violence. And God said to Noah, The end of all flesh has come before Me, for the earth is filled with violence through them; and behold, I will destroy them with the earth."

The end of America as we know it and the beginning of empirical change will be the sign of violence in America. Not riotous activities of looting children, but the full-fledged violent breakdown of society in every city. Not a protest gone bad, but the breakdown of the general public into anarchy to where God must step in to protect the innocents who are left.

As His bride, it is time to make yourself ready. You are the innocent He is looking to protect.

All My Wonders

Intervention with all My Wonders
  You will feign this is absurd
From the first plague to the last
  Hardened hearts and eyes blurred
Every strike of My hammer
  Distinguished action taken
You will know I sit in judgment
  My actions will not be mistaken
Humble, Pray and Turn
  Forsake your wicked ways
And I will forgive and heal your land
  But you will know I AM, Ancient of Days

Yesterday was the first time that I had watched the recorded murder of Mr. George Floyd.

I have a desire to accomplish two things with the writing of this chapter. First, I want to clarify what I believe the Bible and the Spirit of God are forecasting as the last sign before judgment. Secondly, I want to state unequivocally what I believe to be the heart of God with regards to racism.

I believe and have stated in previous chapters that the last sign for the United States and the final notification that devastating nuclear judgment is about to occur in our country will be riots and chaos throughout this great nation. I believe that *what we are experiencing today is a precursor, an earnest of what is to come.* I don't know if the riots and chaos that are coming to our cities, which I believe signal the end of this once great nation, will be racially motivated or not. In fact I believe they will have more to do with the financial crisis and the hyper-depression that we are about to undergo.

Seeing what is happening today though, I tremble at what is in store for our country, the church, and my family. I know beyond a shadow of a doubt that it is going to get progressively worse and we will experience multiple hammer strikes of judgment that will come suddenly in an attempt to jumpstart our hearts into a walk of repentance. Each strike of the hammer will be held by His hand, but be sure it is covered in a velvet glove, meaning that He will grant periods of time for repentance.

Please let this be a wake-up call for you. I beg of you to recognize the message of "Moses" within this plague of Covid-19. I plead that you will see this unrest that is occurring for what it is: an alarm clock to what is coming without national repentance. All of this and what is to come, the hammer strikes of God are interruptions to our sinful lives and natures to arouse us to love Him as He deserves to be loved. To follow Him in the righteousness that only He can give. To arise in the holy nature of Jesus Christ as our substitution to all of this suffering. But without repentance, national and personal, we will be left to our own defense against the wages of sin. Please run to Jesus while there is still time and ask Him to restore your first love.

Racism has been a scourge on this planet since the beginning of time. To think that the racism that is experienced in this country is absent just because the major populace does not have personal experiences with it and prefer to live out a life of oblivion to the suffering of those who do experience it does not mean that it doesn't exist. God sees every single abuse of power even if we don't or refuse to, and this too is under the judging hand of Almighty God.

Take great care in the stance you take through this time to ensure you are not "kicking" against the velvet hand of God holding the hammer of judgment. It is time to rise up on the side of Jesus Christ and oppose anything that is Pharaoh-esque in its abuse of power. This is not the time to hold anything in your heart that even remotely resembles hatred or racism. If you question even for a moment that something remains in you, ask the Holy Spirit to remove it so you are on the side of God. Don't let that "conscience" tug from the Holy Spirit go ignored. Let Him remove all vestiges of hate and lay your pride down and recognize that we all have biases to lay down.

What we are experiencing today is just the beginning of mercies. Get your heart in the right position before God and allow Jesus to free you from any encumbrances to His glory.

I was heartbroken today over our current events and as I lay before God, I released my anguish and honest opinions and feelings before Him. I told Him of my deep love for this country and my intense shame of the man we call president for the actions that I witnessed as they occurred live on television. I expressed to Him the blindness that I see from many Christians who are lifting this man up as their idol and their blatant justification of his overt evil actions.

What had brought me to this place of utter despair before God was the witness of watching legal, peaceful protesters at La Fayette Park in Washington, DC, and the president issuing an ultimatum to the governors of every state to "dominate" the protestors into submission or else he would do it by mobilizing the military. Then suddenly and without warning, lines of police officers in riot gear and some on horses began to push the "lawfully assembled" demonstrators with violent force.

They hurled tear gas and rubber bullets to push them from their position. I assume this was a staged example to demonstrate and to convey to the governors what was expected of them by way of action by domination.

Then to top it all off, he marches across the street for a photo-op with a Bible in hand. I am appalled that not only are Christians supporting this kind of evil blindly, but even "famous" Christian leaders as well. *I am not speaking of their political position; I am speaking of this evil act.*

Then I read articles trying to convince everyone who is a Christian why they should support this president because he is receiving council from famous preachers, and should be extended grace as a new Christian. Well I have news for you, the council he has been given has not worked in four years because he is still an arrogant, egotistical bully and you are validating his actions under some false premise that he is somehow good for Christianity. He has been crowned in many Christian circles as your king and Jesus is weeping. The throne of Jesus Christ is not a booth and neither Donald Trump, Barrack Obama, nor any other national leader gets to rise to a position and sit in His seat.

As I opened the scriptures during my time of prayer, I believe I have seen God's heart for where we are right now as a nation. There was another man who was in charge of a great nation. His name was Pharaoh, and

God saw everything he was doing and he heard every heart-cry of the oppressed, "And the Lord said, I have surely seen the oppression of My people who are in Egypt and have heard their cry because of their taskmasters, for I know their sorrows" (Ex. 3:7). Egypt is a type of the world and in this case, the United States of America. From that point on, God began to send hammer strike judgments in order to bring about repentance. "So I will stretch out My hand and strike Egypt with all My wonders which I will do in its midst" (Ex. 3:20).

Literally God had said that He was going to intervene on behalf of the oppressed and unheard and in doing so, He would send progressive judgments that would be perfectly timed, perfect in duration, and perfect in mercy, and that they would be distinguishing actions, or "My wonders" as He called them on behalf of the people and He would leave no doubt to anyone that these judgments were from Him.

Let there be no doubt that what the United States is experiencing right now is the judgment of God. I hear a lot of misplaced theology today claiming that the evil atrocities occurring today are from the devil or from the evil concoctions of men, but let there be no mistake this plague is from God. I wonder what it is going to take before America and her citizens make their way to their knees and cry out to Him for His mercy. When will Christians lay down their idol worship and get back to their first love. Again, make no mistake, God is sending "His wonders" to the United States in the form of progressive judgments. They will be swift, they will be undeniable, and they will be perfect for His purposes.

When God judged Pharaoh, he did it in this same fashion, repetitiously and rigorously leaving no doubt in anyone's mind who was in fact creating the havoc being experienced and each plague was distinctly unseen before or since. He sent strike after strike after strike and there was no doubt that it was Him trying to free his people from oppression and Idol worship, so too of the United States today.

When God determines that the only recourse for any nation is judgment, He has a hopeful outcome in mind. He does not judge because He is angry. He judges because He is anguished and heartbroken and is being merciful to allow those who will recognize "His wonders" to come back to Him.

Today when evil occurs, we use 2 Chronicles 7:14 as a catchphrase,

> *If My people who are called by My name will humble themselves, and pray and seek My face, and turn from their wicked ways, then I will hear from heaven, and will forgive their sin and heal their land.*

The church needs to wake up to what God is doing before it's too late and our opportunity to act on this scripture departs from us. We sit in church and use this scripture as a prelude to confession on behalf of what others are doing instead of actually doing what this scripture says: humble yourself, pray, turn...then...

There are few humble prayers coming forth today, only accusatory expositions toward what others are doing and there certainly isn't much fruit of repentance. Without "action" accompanying our entreaties before God, the activity of our prayers are meaningless and there will be no hearing from heaven, no forgiveness and no healing of the land.

I hope it is not too late to heed the call of the Spirit to actually activate the benefits of this prayer. If it doesn't occur soon, the next thing we should be looking for is a distinguishing action in the form of a hammer strike of judgment. What has to happen before we will acknowledge that God is trying to get our attention? We have lost our first love and He is weary of hearing the voices of the oppressed.

For Pharaoh, the "My wonders" plagues came in the form of water judgment, livestock judgment, swarms of frogs, flies and lice, not to mention disease and weather judgments. I wonder when we will recognize that much of the "My wonders" plagues have already arrived in the United States in the form of Covid-19, a depressed economy including a shortage of livestock, and yet our hearts are too hardened already to see it and we are committed to either following our idols or our prejudices.

What kind of water judgment or weather judgment must we endure in order to recognize our current condition? God help us if we do not activate 2 Chronicles 7:14 into something other than just a cute catchphrase.

I close with this:

> *Of how much worse punishment, do you suppose, will he be thought worthy who has trampled the Son of God underfoot, counted the blood of the covenant by which he was sanctified a common thing, and insulted the Spirit of Grace? For we know Him who said, Vengeance is Mine, I will repay, says the Lord. And again, The Lord will judge His people. It is a fearful thing to fall into the hands of the living God.*
>
> Hebrews 10:29–31

Do not continue to be or become a cataract Christian whose vision becomes progressively opaque who loses sight of every truth. Our vision is so poor and has been blurred for long enough. Please allow what we are going through as a people to be a surgical removal of that cloudy lens obscuring your sight. Allow this experience to make you more like Him so that all we see are people's hearts appearing on the outside.

> *If My people who are called by My name will humble themselves, and pray and seek My face, and turn from their wicked ways, then I will hear from heaven, and will forgive their sin and heal their land.*
>
> 2 Chronicles 7:14

This scripture has become a catchphrase for the church today. But if you read it for what it truly says, it is calling us to *humble ourselves first* and then pray. So many times, we use this as a jumping off platform to point out everyone else's sins instead of obeying what it requires of us which is to look inward. It's not about what others are doing, it's about me: my sin, my country's sin, and my lack of repentance or turning from sin to God. The prophecy and prayer below are my attempts at obeying God and truly trying to live out this scripture in hopes that maybe it becomes meaningful again.

The chaos that is about to be unleashed on the city streets of America, come *directly* from a hammer strike of judgment from the hand of God, in an *indirect manner*.

The chaos that is about to ensue, is not due to His "direct" involvement. Rather, it is the consequence of God removing His restraining hand and allowing the natural results of men's choices and activities to play out in such a way that they become His judging implement.

The foretelling of future events is not necessarily God condoning nor is He implementing such actions. On the contrary, God foretells in order to call a nation, this nation, to repentance and He will simultaneously hold each side accountable for their extreme actions thus becoming His very own judging implements.

Many in the church today have lost their objectivity, God has not! God has not, will not, and does not take sides in the affairs of men. He stands only on the side of righteousness, His righteousness.

His word for the church in this hour is, "Come away with Me. Come to My perch of objectivity once again and dwell beneath My wings. Do not fall for the subtle lie that is being whispered in your consciousness ('God's on the Republican side,' they say or 'God's on the Democratic side,' they say) *It is all a lie.* I am not created in your image of Me. I am not beholden to any political party as you suspect. My ways are not your ways and My thoughts are not your thoughts," says the Lord.

Without repentance, coming soon to the city streets of America will be rebellious rioting and chaos. This will be His instrument of judgment. The military will be called in and the rioting will be "put down" and defeated with a great slaughter. There will be great loss of life. This too will be His instrument of judgment.

None of these activities of men will be viewed by God as righteous. In the eyes of God, rebellion is as the sin of witchcraft and cannot be eradicated with the military's rage of violence. He sees it all as evil.

Hear the words of the prophet Oded:

> *Look, because the Lord God of your fathers was angry with Judah, (rebellious people) He has delivered them into your hand; (military authority) but you have killed them in a rage that reaches up to heaven...are you not also guilty before the Lord your God? Now hear me, therefore, for the fierce wrath of the Lord is upon you.*
>
> 2 Chronicles 28:9–10

The Lord will ask this question on judgment day, "Are you not both guilty before the Lord?" The fierce wrath of the Lord is upon you. He is now withdrawing His restraining hand; repent before it's too late and seek shelter beneath His wings.

Election Cycle Hammer Judgments

I believe God's message has been clear and has not changed. The time period that we are in is His final warning and call for those who will hear and see. God is judging (present tense), both the winner and loser of this presidential election in one election cycle. Below is a blow-by-blow outline as they have occurred and will continue to occur, that should serve to point this nation to the reality of what is ahead for us if repentance isn't actuated. This cycle will continue until the Most High God, the Lord of Hosts has His way.

Hammer Strikes

Hammer Strike 1
- A disputed election

Hammer Strike 2
- No clear victory and no peace.

Hammer Strike 3
- False Prophets Exposed
  - Lying prophets of news media
  - Lying prophets of social media
  - Lying prophets in the Church: prophesying out of their own minds, parroting each other's voices but not hearing from nor speaking for the Spirit of the living God.

Hammer Strike 4
- The Great Reversal
  - What God is about to do will become known as the Great Reversal. Donald Trump will be

Since he was not - this author should be stoned!

declared the winner of the 2020 Presidential Election. The first will be last and the last first. It will be His undeniable strike of judgment on this corrupt political system fulfilling Isaiah 9:14. He is judging both the loser and winner in this one election cycle.

Hammer Strike 5
- Chaos in American Cities
  - Rioting, chaos, looting, death, and fires.

Hammer Strike 6
- Martial Assault Declared
  - This will be an overreach of military intervention whereby innocent people become collateral damage.

Hammer Strike 7
- God judges wickedness. According to Judges 9, the president will receive a blow to the head and loss of life. God judges the idols of men even when the idols of men are men.

Currently, God is brooding in heaven like a hen at her nest and calling whosoever will, to come beneath the shelter of His wings while there is still time. A new beginning and a great awakening are coming. There will come a great hatching when this is all over. Jesus is about to send forth His ball-peen prophets to break some eggs. A new batch of chicks will come forth and there will be a great awakening of those whose shells were too hard previously and not ready to hear the message of this Elijah-Company.

Lord Jesus,

I am your child and as such I am being called to humble myself before You in personal and national repentance. God, I am sorry that I am being driven at times by my anger. Anger which is turning into bitterness deep inside. I am angered over the abuses of authority, angered over innocent people dying, angered over the murder of an innocent man (George Floyd) by police, angered at myself for not saying enough throughout the years, angered at myself for excusing the abuse in other human beings and I'm angered at our president for not being a humble leader before a Holy God who is obviously judging our nation.

God, I have been a party to the blindness of the plight and oppression of my fellow citizens of other skin pigments and while I don't condone violence, I understand the voice of the unheard speaking out in protest. Jesus,

not innocent!
not righteous!

this isn't about right vs. left, Republican vs. Democrat, or even black vs. white. This is about systemic sin being allowed to run unchecked within our society. The ugliness happening on the streets is just a mirror being held up by Your Hand reflecting what You see on the inside of every one of us. This is a symptom of a deeper issue of not knowing who You are and of disobeying Your Word. We do not understand the nature of Your Holiness and we prefer to walk through our existence in this life on our own and in our own righteousness. We walk every day with a blind man's stick in our hand. Blind to our own sin and yet tapping to find our way by striking at the sins of others. God help us as we are not at a place where we can help ourselves. We are helpless to repair the damage to this nation and I am not speaking of property, I am speaking about people. There is no mask that can protect us from the sin-virus that abides within us, but Jesus You can, and I ask for You to intervene with forgiveness and healing.

Lord, I repent on behalf of myself. I repent for my relatives; I repent for my nation. Lord, I am deeply ashamed of what this has exposed in me and I humble myself before You and ask for You to bring myself and this once great nation to her knees regardless of what You have to do to get us there. Oh God, in judgment remember mercy. Have mercy, O God, as You have promised and remember that we are but dust and that You alone are Holy. You have said that Your mercy will rule the day, so in judgment O Lord, remember mercies.

So, to the God whose very name is holy, set apart from all others. Let Your mercy flow in wave after wave on those who are in awe before You. As Your judgment falls on this nation, remember Your promise and pile on Your mercies and in remembering, pile them high.
In Jesus' name,
Amen.

The Glorified Groom

It's time for preparation
Even for I, the Groom
I go to prepare a place for you
A mansion full of Rooms
I'm anxious to hold your hand again
To gaze into your eyes
I hope you like what I've prepared for you
But I want it to be a surprise

Have you ever wondered what Jesus is doing right now? Many times, I think we envision Him as sitting on His throne and just waiting for the right moment to return and that He really isn't doing much as the Son of Man up in heaven. That somehow, He has ascended to the throne room and has sent down the Holy Ghost as promised and now He is just lingering around as time passes by.

Although He is definitely in a waiting period, the Bible speaks to the activities with which He is engaged in right now which are the preparations for His bride. You see many of the arrangements are already in the works for the marriage to occur. However, there is still activity required by the groom as He anxiously awaits the love of His life. "In My Father's house are many mansions; if it were not so, I would have told you, I go to prepare a place for you" (John 14:2).

Once Jesus arrived in heaven, He sent down the Holy Ghost and then He immediately got to work to prepare Himself for the arrival of His bride. I'm sure He initially presented Himself to the Father as the sacrificial gift required, (I hate to brush over this but it's a book all in itself) and then He got to work preparing the mansions He promised to prepare as well as beginning to lay the groundwork for the marriage supper of the Lamb.

When Jesus left on the day of ascension in Acts 1, He left as the resurrected Christ. At some point, He received the glorified transformation of His entire being just as He prayed, "And now, O Father, glorify Me together with Yourself, with the glory which I had with You before the world was" (John 17:5).

Before Jesus existed as a man, He preexisted as the Word. And as the Word, He had a glory all His own as

HE is continually interceding for us

God which He laid aside to become the Son of Man and die for our sins. When He came back to life as a resurrected man, He ascended to heaven to receive unto Himself once again the glory which He had from the beginning of the world. There have been a handful of saints that have gotten a glimpse of Him in this glorified state.

Isaiah described Him in His previous state as the Word, "...I saw the Lord sitting on a throne, high and lifted up, and the train of His robe filled the temple. So I said: Woe is me, for I am undone!...For my eyes have seen the King, the Lord of Hosts" (Isa. 6:1, 5).

John also describes Him in His current state as the glorified, ascended King:

> Then I turned to see the voice that spoke with me. And having turned I saw...One like the Son of Man, clothed with a garment down to the feet and girded about the chest with a golden band. His head and hair were white like wool, as white as snow, and His eyes like a flame of fire; His feet were like fine brass, as if refined in a furnace, and His voice as the sound of many waters...And when I saw Him, I fell at His feet as dead. But He laid His right hand on me, saying to me, Do not be afraid; I am the First and the Last.
>
> Revelation 1:12–15, 17

So right now, Jesus has received His glorified body and He has begun the promised work of the glorified groom. I can only imagine the anticipation He must feel as He is preparing a permanent place of residence for His espoused. He is literally making ready heaven as promised for His bride. While He is anxiously awaiting His Father's voice to say, "Jesus go and get your bride" and in the meantime He is planning, making, and constructing the perfect habitation for her.

I love Enoch's description of his vision of heaven's habitation.

> *And I saw there as it were a structure built of crystals...and between those crystals tongues of living fire. And my spirit saw the girdle which girt that house of fire, and on its four sides were streams full of living fire, and they girt that house.*
>
> Enoch 71:50

too many quotes of this non-canonical book!

What must the Groom be preparing for His bride? Hallelujah!

I dreamt often before marriage and even now after marriage of a palatial residence that I could design, construct, and abide in with my bride. How must the glorified Carpenter Groom be enjoying His time designing, dreaming, and yes, even constructing His wildest dream home for His beloved. It cannot be imagined what He must be preparing for us as scripture has stated, "But as it is written: Eye has not seen, nor ear heard, nor have entered into the heart of man the things which God has prepared for those who love Him" (1 Cor. 2:9).

As wild as my dreams and schemes and plans get for my bride here on earth, I cannot possibly imagine what God has and is preparing for His bride in heaven. Given the descriptions that have been given to us by saints of old, it's going to be amazing!

You see the tale unfolding of the glorified Groom and His bride is a love story. Jesus is longing for her to be with Him and He is anxiously planning and building and dreaming for the day when He hears His Father say, "It is time."

All things are in place and ready for the Father's perfect timing. Heaven is in hyper-anticipation because every angelic creature has waited for this day. They watch as Jesus rushes to place the finishing touches on each mansion that He himself has designed and created. Every piece of crystal, each piece of furniture, polished with the shine of glory. Everything is in order from the betrothal selection and espousal proceedings. All legal documents are in order and signed in blood. All of the gifts have been given by the groom's representative (The Holy Ghost) and the only thing left now is the final feast and ceremony to be performed.

Jesus has even had His hand in the final feast, as He wants the meal to be perfect for His bride. Each selection according to her tastes and preferences. Because of that, I know there'll be Diet Dr. Pepper at my place setting. I can see Him now agonizing over the table settings, so He is sure that she is happy with His selections.

He must muse to Himself, "The silverware must be gold and not silver, no wait—crystal. It must be crystal, it has to be perfect and I know she loves clear crystal." Like a child at Christmas, He is giddy inside with golden butterflies in His stomach. Then all of a sudden and without warning the glorified Groom hears His Father, "Jesus, go and get your bride...today's Your wedding day."

The glorified Groom jumps to His feet and He looks at Michael the Archangel and says, "How do I look? Do you think she'll remember Me? Do you think she'll still want Me?"

The point I am trying to make is that this is a love story like none other that has ever been told.

Think of this moment. The glorified Groom longing for that instance when He is able to take the hand of His bride. He looks at her so lovingly, trembling with nervous anticipation as He extends His hand to hers to lead her to the final ceremony and feast.

"And if I go and prepare a place for you, I will come again and receive you to Myself; that where I am, there you may be also" (John 14:3). The glorified Groom has prepared a place for me and for you. He has thought about all of the intricate details that would make you and I happy and is ready to be with us forever. He has readied all of heaven and I can hear the angelic spokesman as he speaks with the sound of many waters,

> Gather the people, sanctify the congregation, assemble the elders, gather the children and nursing babes; **Let the glorified Groom** go out from His chamber and the **prepared bride** from her dressing room.
>
> Joel 2:16 (emphasis and name change mine)

The only question that remains is, is she ready for Him? The Bible says that she has prepared herself as well. "Let us be glad and rejoice and give Him glory, for the marriage of the Lamb has come, and His wife has made herself ready" (Rev. 19:7). As far as I can tell, the term of wife in this context has only been used this once and so with it I believe holds some significance. Only those who have made themselves ready will be worthy to wear this label and so it is time to get ready and be the prepared bride. "...And as the bridegroom rejoices over the bride, so shall your God rejoice over you" (Isa. 62:5).

The Prepared Bride

Come my Love and rescue me
I too, myself prepared
Pure for You, innocent and chaste
Wrinkle free, spotless and fair

As the glorified Groom is anxiously waiting for His prepared bride, what is the hold up? What is taking so long? After all Jesus said He was coming soon, but we have long surpassed Webster's definition of "soon," so what's the hold up? He is God and He's a man and so if you say let's go, as a man He's ready! So, what is He waiting for? He is waiting for His bride to be prepared as required and desired.

The church, the body of Christ, and the bride are all used interchangeably and so when Ephesians 5 speaks to husbands regarding their wives, it is implied that the requirements it speaks of toward the church can and should be applied to His bride. "That He might present her to Himself a glorious church, not having spot or wrinkle or any such thing, but that she should be holy and without blemish" (Eph. 5:27).

There is an expectation from the glorified Groom that His bride is just as anxiously readying herself for when He calls to take her hand. While it is true that Christ is coming for a bride who is without spot or wrinkle, the scripture isn't speaking of garments although I am certain she will be spending a lot of time ensuring everything is just perfect with her garments. This scripture's meaning has more to do with speaking to her condition and not her dress. He is looking for a prepared bride who is without moral blemish and the wrinkle spoken of here is not on her clothing, but it is referring to a wrinkle-free face. The original language speaks of this specifically.

When it came to this scripture, I used to always think in terms of it being a goad to the church, the body of Christ, His bride, for her to remove the hinderances causing this unkempt appearance. But the reality is, while it is definitely about purity, it is simultaneously speaking of desire and the anticipated joy of this union.

"Can a virgin forget her ornaments, or a bride her attire?" (Jer. 2:27). When my daughter began preparing herself for her wedding day, it was a sight to behold. She wanted everything to be perfect for this special day. She picked out the perfect dress, and there was no chance that it was going to be allowed to get wrinkled. She and her mother and bridesmaids planned for months every minute detail. She watched her figure; she exercised and ate properly. On the day of the wedding, the ladies went into some sort of hidden ceremony that I don't want to know about or care to explain, but I can tell you everything was attended to. Why did she do this? Why was it important to her? She wanted everything to be perfect for her anxiously waiting groom.

He was ready long before she was and just sitting around with the guys, but not her and her crew. They were primping and powdering and trimming, ensuring everything was going to be perfect. She even made an appointment to have her teeth cleaned. Seriously, her teeth cleaned! The point I'm making is, nobody had to scold her into making sure she was without spot or wrinkle. She wanted it so she required it of herself. She wanted her face to be radiant. And why? Because she desired to please the one she was preparing for so when it was time for them to touch hands at the ceremony, everything was perfect for the man she loved. No spots, no wrinkles, and a face with a special glory to behold.

The same should be true of the bride of Christ. She should be primping, grooming, and yes even cleaning her teeth. Is this the bride you see before you today? Is

the focus is all external!

she the prepared bride the Bible speaks about? I fear it is not so. I have a hard time seeing the blushing bride of purity. She looks more like a harlot being passed around. The glorified Groom is coming back for a prepared bride that hasn't lost her shy innocence but the bride that I see is out shopping for sexy X-rated lingerie. "Can a virgin forget her ornaments, or a bride her attire? Yet My people have forgotten Me days without number" (Jer. 2:32).

Hear the Prayer of a Homeless Savior

"Father, I lay My head down to rest again, alone!
Anguished by the silence of My solitude
Weary from emotional tears of anguish
Hearing only the echoed words of beatitude

So I pray, I pray for those who use Me
I pray for those who say they are mine and are not
I pray for those who have shaken My hand in introduction
Yet their time in My closet a royal boycott

I came, I died, I suffered, I bled
I was buried, risen, ascended
Sending My Gift of Holy Comforter
Only to be ignored and upended

So now I lay Me down to sleep
I pray the Lord My soul to keep
My anguished soul to shake the earth
A tsunami pool of tears I weep

Banished from those I came and died for
They have left Me for a harlot's allure
She making love to prosperity's lust
I sleep alone, a homeless Savior"

As His bride, we have not forgotten Him in the sense that we no longer remember He is around. It's not even a lack of time spent in prayer. No, Jeremiah is saying that she has "ceased to care" to the point of forgetting that her special day is coming and instead of preparing herself like a lovesick bride she is out primping for her lover and doesn't care anymore about the attention required for Him to even want to come back. What groom wants to meet his bride at the altar who has forgotten her ornaments or wearing her unmentionables.

The Father hasn't called for the glorified Groom to go and get His prepared bride yet because she is just a bride and is not prepared. There is no longing for that day nor is there any cry heard with her speaking, "Even so, come glorified Groom." The glorified Groom had every intention of coming "soon," but Webster's definition has to be changed because He is still waiting for

this entire section h been absent of the heart until now

the right girl with a heart that is longing to be united with Him, and she hasn't shown herself prepared. "Then he said to his servants, The wedding is ready, but those who were invited were not worthy" (Matt. 22:8).

It is not about spots and wrinkles though it is. It's about desire! The desire of the bride to so long for her groom that she yearns to prepare herself. The glorified Groom has not been beckoned by His Father yet because He is looking down on this bride and saying, "For I am jealous for you with godly jealousy. For I have betrothed you to one husband, that I may present you as a chaste virgin to Christ" (2 Cor. 11:2).

You see, the timing of this event is in the hands of the Father. He is going to "present" you to His Son as a chaste virgin. It will be on His recommendation to proffer you to the glorified Groom and it is the Father's desire that she be pure from carnality, modest, and chaste in appearance and pure from every fault. Cleaned properly right down to her teeth. A virgin, a marriageable daughter who has abstained from idolatry and kept herself chaste.

Remember when you first fell in love with Jesus? Everything was new, fresh, and exciting. It was like having blurred vision and not knowing it until you put on glasses for the first time. You loved His Word, you desired to spend time with Him, and most of all you weren't afraid to ask Him to cleanse you from anything that was defiling you or wasn't pure. You longed to be in His presence, you couldn't wait to spend time with Him and somehow that love has been lost by looking for another.

Someone or something other than Him has become more important to you, something else is capturing your attention. No Father is going to allow his child to marry someone who is not compatible. If the father sees the espoused having eyes for another, unsure of her commitment to his son, he isn't going to agree to allow this ceremony to take place. He is going to wait for the right girl to come along. The one who only has eyes for his son.

It's time for the bride of Christ to become the prepared bride. Primped, prepared, and longing for her glorified Groom. "Nevertheless I have this against you, that you have left your first love" (Rev. 2:4). Does the Father see a bride longingly preparing for His Son with no eyes for another or does he see a woman who has laid aside her first love?

Allow the word of God, the prophet's voice, the shofar of God in whatever form it comes to you be the maid of honor and/or the mother of the bride to you and allow them to get you ready. Don't be afraid to make yourself ready, be spotless, be wrinkle-free, perfumed, and clean. Be penetrated deeply by the searching eye of the Holy Spirit and ask Him to help you regain that anxious expectation of His arrival.

The glorified Groom is about to break forth in the Eastern sky for His prepared bride. This is not "hide-and-seek" but ready or not here He comes. Are you ready?

Ephesians 5:27 give us an indication of what the Father is looking for in the prepared bride and I believe it will be the key to Him calling to the glorified Groom to go and get His future wife. The word "wrinkle" in the original language refers to a wrinkle "especially on the face" (Strongs 4512). He is looking for a bride that is not only prepared, but has eyes longing for her espoused. Her face is wrinkle-free because she is joyously anticipating the union ceremony and she is looking up to heaven and calling for Him, and the Father hears it so often and so much that He cannot ignore the cries from earth and has to beckon His Son to go and get His prepared bride. Then one day:

> ...the Spirit and the bride say, Come! And let him who hears say, Come! And let him who thirsts come...He who testifies to these things say, Surely I am coming quickly. Amen. Even so, come, Lord Jesus! Let us be glad and rejoice and give Him glory, for the marriage of the Lamb has come, and His wife has made herself ready.
>
> Revelation 22:17, 20; 19:7

Shofar Life or Anesthetized Death

Life or death is in the message
*   Baptized or anesthetized?*
Is laughing gas your discourse
*   Then you'll sleep enough to be euthanized*
Life or death is in the message
*   Baptized or anesthetized?*
Unction with a Life injection
*   Then Satan's plan, capsized*

Before the fall of man, God had allowed man (Adam) to have access to the Tree of Life. "The Lord God planted a garden eastward in Eden, and there He put the man whom He had formed...The tree of life was also in the midst of the garden..." (Gen. 2:8–9).

So, for a time, man had full access to the Tree of Life. It was not God's intended purpose for man to ever die. It was man's sin that caused him to have discontinued access to this life -sustaining nourishment from God. It was an unintended suicide that occurred when they disobeyed the Lord.

Once sin occurred, a punishment was enacted that man could no longer have access to the Tree of Life.

> *Therefore the Lord God sent him out of the garden of Eden...So He drove out the man; and He placed cherubim at the east of the garden of Eden, and a flaming sword which turned every way, to guard the way to the tree of life.*
>
> Genesis 3:23–24

With the loss of access to the Tree of Life, man (Adam) began to die. Without the support of this life-giving sustenance, man could no longer live forever and had to suffer the consequence of his actions.

The next time we see the Tree of Life in scripture, it is in heaven awaiting a reunion of sorts with redeemed mankind.

> *And he showed me a pure river of water of life, clear as crystal, proceeding from the throne of God and of the Lamb. In the middle of its street, and on*

either side of the river, was the tree of life, which
bore twelve fruits, each tree yielding its fruit every
month. The leaves of the tree were for the healing of
the nations.

Revelation 22:1–2

Something to take note of here is that the "Tree of Life" seems to be inextricably connected to the "River of Life." The River of Life seems to be the fountainhead which is indistinguishable in origin and yet feeds the life energy to the Tree of Life and thereby its fruits and healing leaves.

One day very soon, anyone who knows and is having a living relationship with Jesus Christ will be reunited and allowed access once again to this once-forbidden life-giving force of God. However, in the meantime, from the inception of the Genesis punishment to the revelation restoration, the access to this forever life sustenance is supplied only by Jesus Christ the fountainhead through the conduit of His Holy Spirit.

In Genesis, man was separated from the fountain of this forever tree. In Revelation, man is somehow reunited with this miracle of forever life. In the interim, the only access to the scent and sound of this tree can only come from a conduit. You see, Jesus not only is the fountainhead, but He is also the conduit. In fact, He is the only conduit. It is because of Him that any of us are allowed eternal life and access one day to this Tree of Life and River of Life.

This forbidden life tree is waiting for anyone who will accept the truth of the fountainhead of Jesus Christ.

God has given us a unique and holy opportunity. At Christ's death, burial, resurrection, and ascension, He took back His rightful place as fountainhead to the Tree of Life. He is that inextricably linked and indistinguishable source that transfers His forever life as He flows as the River of Life to the Tree of Life to the Fruit of Life and then to us so that we might live forever once again with God in the garden.

No one else on earth can claim that honor. With that honor comes a responsibility of making sure others know the truth in all its glory and God honors us by allowing us to somehow become "surrogate conduits" to His life. A shofar in His hand if you will.

The only life of Jesus that some will ever experience will be because we take our responsibility as surrogate conduit and shofar seriously. God wants to use you and I to blow his message through our beings in the hopes that the sound will reach the Adamic nature in those who come in contact with it and somehow it inspires them to come to the fountainhead, Jesus Christ.

Breath equals life, and God wants to blow the Holy Spirit life through you and I as His shofar (surrogate conduits) to a lost and dying world. The message that

God breathes through the shofar is meant to bring life to those cast out in Genesis and life to those awaiting Revelation. It is meant to be a sustaining breath of life for the lost and the elect.

If Jesus is Life, why is His message going out today and producing less? Instead of sudden bursts of awakening life, we are giving relaxation drugs telling the lost that they are "okay" and everything will be fine with no requirements of repentance. Much of what comes from the pulpit today is the administration of anesthesia. We're not preachers, we're anesthetists. They anesthetize then euthanize. The healing Balm of Gilead does not need an anesthetizing message to lull the people into a relaxed state so that they can feel good about their Christianity. This philosophy of "God has delayed His coming" is over. He is on His way and will no longer postpone His coming. He is imminently on the horizon. Wake up! Don't allow the gas mask of the religious anesthetizer to lull you with their laughing gas and put you to sleep.

God's message was not supposed to change from one generation to the next. Before the first coming of Jesus the message was that a forerunner would come.

Behold, I send My messenger before Your face, who will prepare Your way before You. The voice of one crying in the wilderness: Prepare the way of the Lord; Make His paths straight.

Mark 1:2

John the Baptist's message was a simple one.

"John came baptizing in the wilderness and preaching a baptism of repentance for the remission of sins" (Mark 1:4). Then in verse 14, it says John was put in prison and apparently the way was prepared because his days of preaching were over and Jesus took over, and what was His message?

Now after John was put in prison, Jesus came to Galilee, preaching the gospel of the kingdom of God, and saying, The time is fulfilled, and the kingdom of God is at hand. repent, and believe in the gospel.
Mark 1:14

Before the first coming, so shall the second coming be! Malachi and Isaiah both prophesy that at Christ's coming, forerunner Elijah will come and prepare the way. In a certain sense, Elijah is simply a forerunner's message and it's the same for His second coming as it was for His first. John's message was repent, and Jesus carried on the same message of repentance and that same message of repentance is to be proclaimed today.

Instead of this message of life that springs from repentance, we have espoused a message of death. Anesthetized to be euthanized. Rigor mortis has begun to
set into their bones, "Woe to you, scribes and Pharisees,
hypocrites! For you are like whitewashed tombs which
indeed appear beautiful outwardly, but inside are full
of dead men's bones and all uncleanness" (Matt. 23:27).
I'm sorry if this sounds harsh, but if the lost are to ever
be saved and the elect ever revived, then the rigidity of
this death message must be resurrected to one with life.

There is no time for formalities and rituals, He is
coming! Revival is coming! The river of the Water of
Life is coming, and He wants to flow through the conduit of you and me, but it must be a message of life
springing forth from the fountainhead and producing
repentance.

Joel saw this day coming. He described it as a "season" of rain. He speaks of a former rain (The day of Pentecost with the arrival of the Holy Ghost baptism with
tongues of fire) and a latter rain promised for the final
season. "...For He has given you the former rain faith-
fully, and He will cause the rain to come down for you.
The former rain and the latter rain..." (Joel 2:23).

What a glorious promise to the end-time saints that
such a powerful rain is coming that it will cause a har-
vest indescribable. It will be accompanied with dreams,

visions, and prophetic words, and to top it all off it's for everyone.

> *And it shall come to pass afterward that I will pour out My Spirit on all flesh; Your sons and your daughters shall prophesy, Your old men shall dream dreams, your young men shall see visions...I will pour out My Spirit in those days. And I will show wonders in the heavens and in the earth: Blood and fire and pillars of smoke. The sun shall be turned into darkness, and the moon into blood, Before the coming of the great and awesome day of the Lord. And it shall come to pass that whoever calls on the name of the Lord shall be saved.*
>
> Joel 2:28–32

Ezekiel envisioned this day also and his description sounds sort of like the rains are bursting over its boundaries and joyfully flooding the area with enough water to swim in. Can you imagine that? Such a move of God that it brings so much joy and energy and life. Everybody jumping for joy, playing in the waters of life. He describes it much better than I:

> *Then he brought me back to the door of the temple; and there was water, flowing from under the threshold of the temple...the water was flowing...*

when the man went out...he measured...the water
came up to my ankles...Again he measured...the
water came up to my knees...Again he measured...
the water came up to my waist.

Ezekiel 47:1–4

Ever since the former rain, the day of Pentecost when the Holy Spirit was originally poured out, His outpouring waters have continued to increase over time. Many societies have experienced these outpourings in measure. We have seen throughout the ages this water flow from the temple of God up to the ankles in the first two American awakenings. Up to the knees in the outpouring on the country of Wales and even today, there are many other outpourings that come up to the waist like China's current underground church or Russia's former underground church.

I believe what is promised to us is an even greater outpouring than anything we have read about in the past or experienced in the present. "Again he measured...and it was a river that I could not cross; for the water was too deep, water in which one must swim" (Ez. 47:5).

I have heard and read about a lot of revivals, but I have never truly experienced one. I have seen the Holy Spirit move in measure and I have seen some foolishness that masqueraded itself as a move of God, but what I see being promised isn't something that can be counterfeited. Oh, the enemy will try. There is always a chlorine pool somewhere to swim in, but the life-giving water will be unmistakable, and it will be waters to swim in.

I can't fathom what must be coming to us, but I do know this, it will be teaming with fish and healings and no anesthesia needed, thank you Jesus!

> *He said to me, "Son of man, have you seen this?" Then he brought me and returned me to the bank of the river. And it shall be that every living thing that moves, wherever the rivers go, will live. There will be very great multitude of fish, because these waters go there; for they will be healed, and everything will live wherever the river goes.*
> Ezekiel 47:6, 9

I can't stop thinking about it...salvation and healing. People being made whole again by the power of the life-giving river that is Jesus Christ.

One last word of loving warning for you if you are already a Christian. When this revival takes place, don't be wearing that golden calf necklace. One golden calf around your neck while swimming in revival waters is not sustainable. You'll play in the waters for a while but eventually you'll succumb to the exhaustion of carrying around this extra weight and it will become a self-inflicted judgment. Multiple golden calves around the neck and attempting to participate in the revival waters will result in certain death. Nobody can survive such arrogance and the result will be a self-inflicted judgment of death by drowning or rather death by idol fixation or shall I say idol asphyxiation?

Don't get into the waters without removing your idols. Swim free! Don't let anything weigh you down and play in the stream of God with the enjoyment intended. It's a dangerous place to swim with hidden idols in your pockets. Repent and live!

Board Meeting of Prophets

Voice of the prophets
The message has not changed
Even in the board room
Nothing gets rearranged

"I want to call this meeting to order" come the words of the president. "Isaiah, can you read the minutes of the last meeting?"

"But sir, are you sure? They're quite long?"

"Just follow protocol, please, and read..." quipped President Worthy.

"Ah yes sir, if you insist."

Isaiah begins, "In the beginning God created the heavens and the earth..." (Gen. 1:1).

"Okay, okay, I get it...stop. If everyone agrees that they have read ahead and are up to date with the current signs of the times on earth, we can proceed with the next order of business. All in favor say, 'Jesus is worthy.'"

All respond with enthusiasm, "Jesus is worthy!"

James leans over and whispers to John his brother, "Whew thank the Lord, I'm not sure I could stay awake during that Old Testament litany of names..."

President Worthy responds, "Jimmy, I can hear you, you know? Remember what I told you the last time."

"Yes sir," James responds, "taming the tongue."

President Worthy begins the meeting by saying, "There is only one item on the agenda this evening, so if nobody objects, I'd like to get right at it by posing a simple question around the room. What is the message the United States of America needs to hear right now and how do I convince them of their need for Me? They have forsaken Me and have been following their idols for years and it's time to send a clear message to her."

Abruptly, everyone begins talking at once to the point that nobody is being heard.

"Silence!" speaks President Worthy, interrupting the chaotic thundering of their many prophetic voices. "Let's do this with some dignity shall we? Let's just go around the room. Obviously, I cannot hear from everyone so I will call upon you to speak one at a time and please nobody interrupt."

"Jeremiah" President Worthy says. "You have been sitting there silently, but you obviously have something to say given the tears cascading down your cheek. Are you all right?"

"Yes sir," Jeremiah replies, "This just seems so familiar to me that I can feel the weight of the burden deeply within me."

"I wouldn't expect anything less from you, My son. Just tell Me what message you would declare to America at this time."

Jeremiah begins, "Well sir, I guess I would have to echo some of my past declarations, and I would probably just restate them. They have to understand that requirements and consequences do not change and so I would declare it like this:

> *Thus says the Lord: "I remember you, the kindness of your youth, the love of your betrothal, when you went after Me in the wilderness...Nevertheless I have this against you, that you have left your first love."*
>
> Jeremiah 2:2, Revelation 2:5

"Hey, wait a minute that's mine!" exclaims John

President Worthy responds, "Ah no, actually John, that's Mine. Stop interrupting. Go on Jerry..."

"Yes sir," John whispers sheepishly.

Jeremiah begins again, "I guess then I would have to remind them of their journey by saying:

I brought you into a bountiful country, to eat its fruit and its goodness. But when you entered, you defiled My land and made My heritage an abomination. And then I think we need to remind them that while during Your absence...The priests did not say, "Where is the Lord? And those who handle the law did not know Me; The rulers transgressed against Me; The prophets prophesied by Baal, and walked after things that do not profit."

Therefore I will yet bring charges against you, says the Lord...Has a nation changed its gods, which are not gods? But My people have changed their Glory for what does not profit. For My people have committed two evils: They have forsaken Me, the fountain of living waters, and have dug their own wells that can hold no water.

Have you not brought this on yourself, in that you have forsaken the Lord your God when He led you in the way? Your own wickedness will correct you, and your backslidings will rebuke you. Know therefore and see that it is an evil and bitter thing that you have forsaken the Lord your God, and the fear of Me is not in you, says the Lord God of hosts.

Jeremiah 2:7–8; 11,13; 17, 19

"Did you get all of that, Isaiah?" asks President Worthy.

"Yes sir, but Jeremiah is sitting too close...he's getting my scroll stained with tears."

"All right, all right that's enough."

"Zeke, I guess you're next. What would you say to this nation that has turned away from righteousness and knowing that if they do not turn back to Me, a fiery indignation awaits them?"

"Well, it's pretty simple for me sir. I would say,"

I will judge you...every one according to his ways, says the Lord God. Repent, and turn from all your transgressions, so that iniquity will not be your ruin. Cast away from you all the transgressions which you have committed, and get yourselves a new heart and a new spirit. For why should you die?...For I have no pleasure in the death of one who dies, says the Lord God. Therefore turn and live! Then I looked, and behold, a whirlwind was coming out of the north, a great cloud with raging fire engulfing itself and brightness was all around it and radiating out of its midst like the color of amber, out of the midst of the fire.

Ezekiel 18:30–32, 1:4

President Worthy looks at Ezekiel, "Are you sure you want to be that explicit?"

Ezekiel looks down at his hands and after a solemn pause he says, "Yes sir, absolutely!"

The president begins again, "All right let's see, Elijah...No wait. I don't think I need you to weigh in on this. I have a special assignment for you later and I don't want your mind or heart distracted"

"Isaiah, are you getting all of this in the minutes? I want to make sure I can review each of these proclamations later."

"Oh yes, Sir, every word."

"Okay well, I want to hear from you next, Isaiah. Can you speak your heart to this issue and document it later?"

"Absolutely sir, I learned the importance of this to you a long time ago when you told me to "Take a large scroll, and write on it with a man's pen concerning... these matters" (Isa. 8:1).

"All right then, let's go on."

"Well sir, I really think we should try and keep this as positive as possible given their Laodicean proclivities."

"Eww, he thinks now just because he is the minute-taker that he needs to use big words, like 'proclivities,'" comes the snarky comment from Thomas.

President Worthy interrupts, "That's enough, go on Isaiah..."

"Well, sir, I believe I too would keep it simple and positive and even though destruction is coming, there is hope and so I think I would start by saying, "And it shall come to pass in that day that the remnant of this nation...As such as has escaped...will never again depend on him who defeated them, but will depend on the Lord, the Holy One of Israel, in truth. The remnant will return, the remnant of this nation to the Mighty God...A remnant of them will return; The destruction decreed shall overflow with righteousness. For the Lord God of hosts will make a determined end in the midst of all the land."

"Thank you, Isaiah I appreciate your perspective. I will definitely take this into consideration as well," encourages President Worthy.

President Worthy looks past Moses and begins to speak to Peter. "Peter..."

Moses interrupts, "Hey, what about me...You went right by me..."

"I am sorry, Moses, but I already know what you think but to be honest, I need some New Testament right now."

Half the room chuckles and the other half scowls. You can just about guess which did what.

"Peter, let's hear some New Testament proclamation on this subject."

(margin, handwritten) Many make the mistake of substituting the us. for Israel

"Well, sir," Peter begins, "I think I would begin by explaining that 'prophecy never came by the will of man, but holy men of God spoke as they were moved by the Holy Spirit.' And then I think I would have to remind them that in the history of mankind, that 'if God did not spare the angels who sinned, but cast them down to hell and delivered them into chains of darkness, to be reserved for judgment.'"

Jude speaks up, "Pardon me, I don't mean to interrupt but that has always been a little hard to understand. Are you sure you want to start with that?"

President Worthy steps in and says, "This is Peter's message it needs to come from his heart, not yours. You'll have a chance if there's time, Jude. Go on, Pete."

As I was saying:

And did not spare the ancient world, but saved Noah, one of eight people, a preacher of righteousness, bringing in the flood on the world of the ungodly; and turning the cities of Sodom and Gomorrah into ashes, condemned them to destruction, making them an example to those who afterward would live ungodly; and delivered righteous Lot, who was oppressed by the filthy conduct of the wicked.

Therefore, since all these things will be dissolved, what manner of persons ought you to be in holy

*conduct and godliness, looking for and hastening
the coming of the day of God, because of which the
heavens will be dissolved, being on fire, and the
elements will melt with fervent heat? Therefore,
beloved, looking forward to these things, be diligent to be found by Him in peace, without spot and
blameless.*

2 Peter 1:21, 2:4–7, 3:11–12, 14

"Thank you, Pete, I appreciate your perspective as well." President Worthy looks over and sees Thomas shaking his head and he says, "Tommy, what's wrong?"

"Nothing sir, I just can't believe this is happening! I mean I know it's happening, and I believe it without a shadow of a doubt...I just feel what many will feel when they hear this message for the first time."

Ezekiel chimes in, "Yes but we must tell them, we cannot arrive on that final day with blood on our hands."

Thomas assents with a nod, "I know, I know... it's just hard to believe we're here already."

President Worthy interrupts the conversation. "All right, let's move on." Paul, I believe I'd like to hear from you next."

"Hey, what about me?" exclaims Thomas "He practically wrote the whole New Testament and I didn't even get a page. I have an opinion too you know, why are You passing over me again?"

"Trust Me," President Worthy replies, "I already know what you think but fine... Paul has had his moment. Johnny, how about you, let's finish up with this last one."

Well sir, very frankly I would speak a message of love and judgment by saying:

> *Do not love the world or the things of the world. If anyone loves the world, the love of the Father is not in him. For all that is in the world-the lust of the flesh, the lust of the eyes, and the pride of life-is not of the Father but is of the world. And the world is passing away, and the lust of it; but he who does the will of God abides forever. Little children, it is the last hour; and as you have heard that the Antichrist is coming, even now many antichrists have come, by which we know that it is the last hour.*
>
> 1 John 2:15–18

And then honestly sir, I would speak with them with all of the love in my heart that I could muster and tell them to:

> *Come out of her, my people, lest you share in her sins, and lest you receive of her plagues. For her sins have reached to heaven, and God has remembered her iniquities. In the measure that she glori-*

fied herself and lived luxuriously in the same mea-
sure give her torment and sorrow; for she says in
her heart, 'I sit as queen, and am no widow, and
will not see sorrow.' Therefore her plagues will
come in one day-death and mourning and famine.
And she will be utterly burned with fire, for strong
is the Lord God who judges her.

Revelation 18:4–5,7–8

President Worthy looks around the somber room. "Thank you, elders. I believe I have heard enough. Isaiah, if you could finalize the scroll of minutes and get them back to Me, I will then make My decision when the time is right what My message will be. Let us adjourn with a final word of prayer."

The Prayer of a Shofar

Oh God, there are so many names by which I might address you. Elohim, El Shaddai, Jehovah and even my favorite of all YWHW or I Am. You are the Most High God, Glorified Christ enthroned as the Lamb-Lion. There is none worthy to approach your Holy Place except Jesus bid them come. I of all sinners am the least worthy to be accepted into Your presence and yet...Jesus. You take me by Your blood, and You lead me to Your throne as if I somehow belong there and yet somehow I do and it's all because of Jesus. The glorified Messiah King. Crowned once again with the glory with which You wore in the age eternal.

Hear my prayer, oh God. Not just the words that I speak but the aching within me that is unutterable and crushing. I am but frail flesh and blood trying to convey silent spirit impressions that scream to my inner man. Thy voice shakes my soul and my bones tremble with a holy reverent fear. Oh God, how does this flawed existence of a man transmit and convey the truth of your dispatch? Please Lord, broadcast the truth of your message through me. Cover me so thoroughly in Thy blood that the only thing left to be heard is the sound of your breath.

You have given me a high and holy calling that I am unworthy to answer and stand afraid but for the blood that was shed at the cross on my behalf. The vision of Your burden and the conveyance thereof is too great for me! I am an imperfect vessel with flawed language, and flawed tongue and I fear that I may taint and bring harm to Your message and in doing so harm to You and harm to its hearers. And yet, oh God, I must deliver myself of this burden, this message and this vision that you have given me, that I might be delivered from bloodstained hands. That I may stand before You one day with clean hands and a pure heart.

Lord, I have stood in Your presence and You have shown me that which was and is and is to come. I have felt the undone nakedness that only comes with the glaring brightness of Your glory and though imperfect as I am, I cannot deny that I have seen God. Not with mine eyes but with my spirit broken with hot tears and a burdened soul for what is to come. I have been unable to stand in Your presence or glory as my reflection from Your shining countenance is a shame to behold.

I thank Thee, my God, for the covering that is the blood of Jesus Christ that conceals my inadequacies and my iniquities. That I am granted the honor of standing in Your glory cloud though trembling of soul for its awful splendor. Frail flesh trying to convey spiritual impressions from Thy holy presence in a way that can be grasped in the grip of full repentance. Jesus, You are the Great Orator, the Golden Trumpeter who alone is worthy to breathe out the truth of who You are. May I be a useful instrument, a dead tusk in Your hand whom You choose to breathe Your life through. Your breath message is truly the only thing that matters now.

Dark days are ahead for anyone not walking in repentance before You, but there are also glorious days ahead for Your body, Your bride the church. I am excited to see what is in store for Your bride. I am anxious to see the glories You will perform in these last days. And even though Your judgments must fall, it is for Your determined purposes. Though the earth trembles and the fires roar, You stand Lord over them all. May this be the time that Your bride becomes so enamored with You that she wants to so prepare herself as that unspotted, unwrinkled attraction that her groom cannot but wait to see her. May the outcry of her voice be so great that You cannot help but break forth from heaven's throne to meet Your bride in the air. As we cry out for the day of our consummation, though they be filled with dark times, please burn within us that ever-yearning heart's cry: Even so, come Lord Jesus!

Conclusion: Final Scroll of Minutes

Thus says the Lord: I remember you, the kindness of your youth, the love of your betrothal, when you went after Me in the wilderness...Nevertheless I have this against you, that you have left your first love.

Jeremiah 2:2, Revelation 2:5

I brought you into a bountiful country, to eat its fruit and its goodness. But when you entered, you defiled My land and made My heritage an abomination. The priests did not say, Where is the Lord? And those who handle the law did not know Me; The rulers transgressed against Me; The prophets prophesied by Baal, and walked after things that do not profit.

Jeremiah 2:7–8

Therefore I will yet bring charges against you, says the Lord...Has a nation changed its gods, which are not gods? But My people have changed their Glory for what does not profit. For My people have committed two evils: They have forsaken Me, the fountain of living waters, and have dug their own wells that can hold no water.

Jeremiah 2:9, 11, 13

Have you not brought this on yourself, in that you have forsaken the Lord your God when He led you in the way? Your own wickedness will correct you, and your backslidings will rebuke you. Know therefore and see that it is an evil and bitter thing that you have forsaken the Lord your God, and the fear of Me is not in you, says the Lord God of hosts.

Jeremiah 2:17, 19

I will judge you...every one according to his ways, says the Lord God. Repent, and turn from all your transgressions, so that iniquity will not be your ruin. Cast away from you all the transgressions which you have committed, and get yourselves a new heart and a new spirit. For why should you die?...For I have no pleasure in the death of one who dies, says the Lord God. Therefore turn and live! Then I looked, and behold, a whirlwind was coming out of the north, a great cloud with raging fire engulfing itself and brightness was all around it and radiating out of its midst like the color of amber, out of the midst of the fire.

Ezekiel 18:30–32, 1:4

And it shall come to pass in that day that the remnant of this nation...As such as has escaped...will never again depend on him who defeated them, but will depend on the Lord, the Holy One of Israel, in truth. The remnant will return, the remnant of this nation to the Mighty God...A remnant of them will return; The destruction decreed shall overflow with righteousness. For the Lord God of hosts will make a determined end in the midst of all the land."
Prophecy never came by the will of man, but holy men of God spoke as they were moved by the Holy Spirit. If God did not spare the angels who sinned, but cast them down to hell and delivered them into chains of darkness, to be reserved for judgment;...and did not spare the ancient world, but saved Noah, one of eight people, a preacher of righteousness, bringing in the flood on the world of the ungodly; and turning the cities of Sodom and Gomorrah into ashes, condemned them to destruction, making them an example to those who afterward would live ungodly; and delivered righteous

Lot, who was oppressed by the filthy conduct of the wicked.

Therefore, since all these things will be dissolved, what manner of persons ought you to be in holy conduct and godliness, looking for and hastening the coming of the day of God, because of which the heavens will be dissolved, being on fire, and the elements will melt with fervent heat? Therefore, beloved, looking forward to these things, be diligent to be found by Him in peace, without spot and blameless.

2 Peter 1:21; 2:4¬–7; 3:11–12; 14

Do not love the world or the things of the world. If anyone loves the world, the love of the Father is not in him. For all that is in the world-the lust of the flesh, the lust of the eyes, and the pride of life-is not of the Father but is of the world. And the world is passing away, and the lust of it; but he who does the will of God abides forever. "Little children, it is the last hour; and as you have heard that the Antichrist is coming, even now many antichrists have come, by which we know that it is the last hour.
1 John 2:15–18

Come out of her, my people, lest you share in her sins, and lest you receive of her plagues. For her sins have reached to heaven, and God has remem-

bered her iniquities. In the measure that she glori-
fied herself and lived luxuriously in the same mea-
sure give her torment and sorrow; for she says in
her heart, 'I sit as queen, and am no widow, and
will not see sorrow.' Therefore her plagues will
come in one day-death and mourning and famine.
And she will be utterly burned with fire, for strong
is the Lord God who judges her."

Revelation 18:4–5,7–8

"And He said to me, It is done! I am the Alpha and the Omega, the Beginning and the End" (Rev. 21:6).

Epilogue

As a nation, being in covenant with God does not guarantee immunity from consequence or punishment. On the contrary, being in covenant means that we have agreed to terms of said covenant and as such are subject to the blessings and curses of His covenant. Being a nation established in covenant with God does not make that nation immune from His judgments any more than a father can deny punishment to his child.

Immunity of a wayward child guarantees a much harsher punishment in the future. An unrestrained and undisciplined child becomes a wayward man standing before a judge awaiting a much stiffer penalty. Being a nation established in covenant with Almighty God guarantees that breaking covenant with Him requires His hand of justice. There is no such thing as immunity in the kingdom of God in the midst of unrestrained sin. Repentance is required.

A good father initiates discipline as a goad for repentance. The judgment of God is a mercy from a good father, meant to provoke a nation toward repentance, so that a much harsher penalty isn't exacted by another in the future.

We are living in a unique time whereby God has slammed the door on this nation and yet it is wide open. We are at the moment of choice, just before the door latches or the wind blows strong enough to hold it open. The outcome of the door's resting place lies in the choices we make after this to enter in or to walk away.

He is about to move in power. Do not be afraid but trust Him at His Word. His compassions never fail, and His mercy will rule the day. Guard your heart, steel your mind, and trust that at the end of the day, He will have accomplished His good and perfect purpose. But be sure of this, He will have His day and the only safe place is in the shelter of His will.

"For the people do not turn to Him who strikes them, nor do they seek the Lord of Hosts. Therefore the Lord will cut off head and tail...palm branch and bulrush in one day" (Isa. 9:13–14).

There is only one remaining hope for this nation and His name is Jesus. In prayer, I asked God, "Lord, what can I say to touch your heart the way You have touched mine whenever You speak a word to me?"

As I sat in silence for a moment in quiet reflection, I began again to speak and I said, "Jesus..." The Holy

Spirit gently touched me with His manifest presence, and He said, "You just did."

Hallelujah! The name above every name, the name to which every knee shall bow, the name and one word that moves the very heart of God...*Jesus!* Bow to Him today in repentance, He is the only way.

About the Author

I am a student of the Word of God and an aspiring author, but mostly I am a bondservant of the Master. I hold my ministerial credentials through AEGA and I am the president of a non-profit called LifeBack Ministries, the purpose of which lies in the name: to lead anyone who will follow to a place of enablement to get their "LifeBack" in Jesus Christ.

I am like Amos in the Old Testament, a simple shepherd. Not a prophet, or seer, nor any such thing. However, I have been called to walk the rampart as one of His many watchmen. I carry my shofar with me at all times in the hope that I may save some and warn many.

—Rory Larsen

To request a speaking engagement, I can be reached by email at *RoryLarsen@minister.com*.

CPSIA information can be obtained
at www.ICGtesting.com
Printed in the USA
FSHW022109130321

9 781637 691069